GAMBLING
CRIME OR RECREATION?

INFORMATION PLUS
WYLIE, TEXAS 75098
© 1979, 1980, 1982, 1986, 1990, 1992, 1994
ALL RIGHTS RESERVED

EDITORS:
MARK A. SIEGEL, Ph.D.
ALISON LANDES, B.A.
CAROL D. FOSTER, M.L.S.

CHAPTER I

GAMBLING — AN AMERICAN TRADITION

COLONIAL PASTIME

Gambling was a popular pastime in North America even before there was a United States. By the end of the 17th century, just about every county seat in colonial America had a lottery wheel. Playing cards and dice were brought over by both the British and the Dutch. Cockfighting flourished throughout the colonies, especially in the South. Bear-baiting was also a popular sport, but the Puritans banned it, "not because it gave pain to the bear, but because it gave pleasure to the spectators." While strict New Englanders considered gambling a "disorder to God" and levied fines and whippings against gamblers, gambling was much less of a moral issue in other parts of the country.

European visitors to America, from English soldiers during the Revolutionary War period to Frances Trollope in the 19th century, commented on the American's affinity for gambling. George Washington was an avid, though mediocre, card player and wisely limited his betting. Benjamin Franklin printed and sold playing cards. The controversial Stamp Act levied a one-shilling tax on every pack of cards, raising perhaps as much ire as the tax on tea, since every well-furnished colonial home possessed a card table. In the South, the planter-aristocrat, with his thoroughbred horses and imported English furniture, had the opportunity and the wealth to enjoy leisure time pursuits, of which horse racing was a favorite.

During the Colonial Period, lotteries were a popular means of raising funds. English lotteries provided most of the funding to establish the colony of Virginia, and the original Jamestown settlement was financed by a lottery conducted by the Virginia Company in London, England. In 1748, young Ben Franklin organized a lottery to pay for military supplies to defend Philadelphia from attack by Indian tribes and French soldiers. In 1777, to help finance the Revolutionary War, the Continental Congress held a $5 million lottery. Unfortunately, all winnings over $50 were to be paid in promissory notes (to be collected at some future date). The lottery was mismanaged and several scoundrels abused the trust of their fellow revolutionaries. The lottery was a disaster and most people holding winning tickets never received a payoff.

Lotteries were also held to raise money for county treasuries, build bridges, assist churches and schools, and establish relief funds. Lottery proceeds contributed to the establishment of such prestigious Ivy League schools as Harvard, Yale, Columbia, Princeton, and Dartmouth.

ENTERTAINMENT DURING THE JACKSONIAN ERA

President Andrew Jackson believed that a person's destiny should be controlled by the individual, rather than by elected officials. During his administration (1829-1837), popularly known as the era of "the common man," gambling was a form of entertainment enjoyed by large numbers of people, as well as public officials. President Jackson was an avid gambler (he once reportedly bet all of his clothes during a game of chance). During his presidential campaign, Jackson's eventual successor, Martin Van Buren, wagered a new suit, along with $40,000, on his victory in the elections.

During this period, Americans were well-known for their eager and continued interest in all forms of gambling. A Northern traveler in the South commented on the heavy betting at cockfights, which were attended by people from all levels of society. A flatboat merchant who plied the Ohio River observed that Kentuckians were completely absorbed in horse racing and gambling. One could hardly talk to a Kentuckian, he wrote, without hearing the phrase, "I'll bet you."

Along the Mississippi and Ohio Rivers, notorious gamblers earned their keep on the riverboats that sailed down the rivers to New Orleans, a gambler's paradise. The first formal casino in New Orleans opened in 1827, and it soon became a model for other "carpet joints," as the lavishly decorated casinos were called. Riverboat gambling continued after the Civil War, but never regained its ante-bellum (pre-Civil War) dash and glamour.

Urban areas were also centers of gambling activity during the Jacksonian Era. While the countryside and riverfront facilities relied on visitors from outlying areas to attend their cockfights, horse races, or casinos, urban areas had a ready-made customer base. New York City was an early gambling center. By 1850, it had approximately 6,000 flourishing gambling houses, an astounding ratio of one gambling house for every 85 New Yorkers.

THE REFORM MOVEMENT

During the 1840s, a reforming spirit swept across America. Societies formed to combat tobacco use, profanity, and the transit of mail on Sunday. The first woman's rights movement was organized, and temperance crusaders preached against alcohol use. The abolitionist movement against slavery gained significant momentum during these years.

Many reformers attacked gambling. They were most successful in their fight against the flourish-ing lottery business. During the 1830s, some newspapers began publishing accounts of corrupt lotteries and their harmful effect on individuals who could not really afford to buy tickets, but did so anyway. As a result of this negative publicity, lottery permits decreased and lotteries were abolished altogether in most Northern states by 1840. The increasing rate of profiteering by lottery middlemen eventually incited public indignation in the South and West as well. By 1860, every state in the nation except Delaware, Kentucky, and Missouri had enacted constitutional or statutory prohibitions against lotteries.

Although illegal in most states by this time, gambling occurred openly in such cities as New York, Chicago, and New Orleans. In reaction to reform efforts, operators of gambling establishments fought to save their lucrative businesses by paying members of local police forces for protection. Policemen staged pre-arranged raids for appearance's sake, but they were careful not to damage furniture, and they usually returned the gamblers to their places of business after booking them. The very fact that gambling was illegal seemed to add to its popular appeal as an exciting form of entertainment. Attempts to legalize gambling probably would have been opposed by gamblers, operators, and corrupt police and public officials alike.

During the mid- and late-1860s, the financial demands of the Civil War and Reconstruction once again created an interest in lotteries in the southern and western states. However, because of their reputation for breeding corruption and a lack of uniform state regulation, federal legislation against lotteries was introduced. Lottery operators mounted efforts to circumvent anti-lottery laws by forming "gift companies" which operated in essentially the same manner as a lottery.

THE WILD WEST — HONKY-TONKS AND THE GOLD RUSH

The opening of the Far West during the mid-1880s gave gambling in America a second life. Far from both government controls and the moral in-

3

terference of reform groups in the East, gambling became so popular and widespread that monte (a card game) tables were often set up on the street in the middle of town. Professional gamblers, rumored to earn as much as $20,000 per month, were glad to relieve hard-working miners of their gold nuggets. Losses were usually taken philosophically. For the lucky miners, a quick return to their gold mines in the hills would usually replenish whatever they lost at the gaming tables. Gambling houses could easily be found in Kansas City, Dallas, Denver, and San Francisco, as well as nearly every small town located near mining camps, railroad towns, and major cattle trails.

THE LOUISIANA LOTTERY

As noted above, dishonesty and fraud were common in lottery operations during the 1800s. The Louisiana Lottery, however, took these characteristics to such extremes that, by the turn of the century, gambling and political corruption would be forever linked in the minds of many people.

In 1864, 1868, 1872, and 1876, federal laws were passed to stop the expansion of lotteries by taxing them and limiting the activities they could conduct by federal mail. Louisiana was the only state still operating a lottery. In 1865, a New-York-based gambling syndicate* applied for approval to operate a lottery in Louisiana. In return for granting a sales monopoly to the syndicate, the Louisiana state treasury would receive $40,000 annually for 25 years to finance the Charity Hospital in New Orleans. The use of profits from gambling for charitable causes became an established tactic to ensure the acceptance of gambling within the community.

The approval of the Louisiana lottery was assured by rigged elections that kept out candidates opposed to the lottery and by bribing legislators to grant licenses. From its inception, the Louisiana Lottery controlled legislatures, newspapers, banks,

and governors. It continued operating despite prohibitions by federal laws because enforcement officials would not prosecute lottery mangers. Players around the country participated in the Louisiana Lottery by mail, bringing the Lottery's profits to an average $13 million per year, a huge sum of money at the time.

Mounting Criticism

National criticism grew as the Louisiana Lottery extended into every state, with the syndicate receiving more than 90 percent of its income from outside Louisiana. Reformers, labor and farm organizations, newspapers, and churches all requested federal action against the Louisiana Lottery. As a result, the state legislature cancelled the lottery, but using the considerable number of dollars at its disposal, the syndicate forced an extension through a Louisiana constitutional convention.

Finally, in 1890, the U.S. Congress passed legislation banning postal delivery of all items dealing with lotteries and prohibiting the conduct of operations through an agent or representative, such as the New Orleans National Bank. For the first time, violations of this law became punishable by imprisonment. A new provision was also enacted making the offense triable by a court in any jurisdiction through which lottery material had been transported, thereby making it harder to avoid conviction by bribing local jurors.

The Louisiana Lottery Company moved to Honduras in Central America to avoid postal regulations. In 1895, Congress authorized the Postmaster General to withhold delivery of lottery-related mail, and to deny any person representing a lottery company the use of the postal service. Interstate transportation of lottery materials and the use of express mail became illegal in 1895. The anti-lottery laws deprived the Louisiana Lottery Company of the methods by which it had evaded

---

* A syndicate is a group of individuals or corporations formed to undertake an activity, usually one that requires substantial financial backing.

state and federal laws for years and it closed. The combined effect of several federal statues enacted between 1890 and 1895 eliminated lotteries for the next 70 years.

THE PROGRESSIVE ERA
A SECOND PERIOD OF REFORM

Between 1900 and 1917, a reform-minded group of people called the "Progressives" dedicated itself to exposing corruption in big business and municipal governments, correcting social evils, and improving living conditions for women, children, and the poor. Progressive reformers had two main goals: to use state power to curb unscrupulous business trusts and to stem the threat of socialism.

Reformers attacked red-light (prostitution) districts, saloons, and alcoholism. Francis E. Willard founded the Anti-Saloon League to crusade against these establishments, considered to be dominated by crooked city officials and political bosses who supported "booze interests," counted poker chips by night, and miscounted ballots by day. Progressive reformers were instrumental in closing gambling houses and race tracks, as well as policy and bookmaking operations. By 1915, only seven states permitted horse racing.

ORGANIZED CRIME

In 1920, Congress instituted Prohibition, which outlawed the manufacture, transportation, and sale of alcoholic liquors in the United States. However, it could not curb Americans' appetite for alcohol. With its potential for huge profits, the sale of alcoholic beverages became the domain of the underground world of "gangsters," a popular name for criminals. Subsequently, organized crime moved onto other profitable and illicit activities such as gambling.

During the Prohibition Era (1920-1933), illegal gambling was organized into an authoritarian regional and national system. Responsibility for the syndication of gambling is usually attributed to Arnold Rothstein (1881-1928) who invented the inner-city layoff (in which gambling organizations

in one city helped those in other cities cover heavy, potentially risky, bets). Rothstein is also known for masterminding the "Black Sox" Scandal in which the White Sox threw the 1919 World (Baseball) Series to the Cincinnati Reds to assure gambling profits.

Organized crime no longer possesses the glamorous reputation it enjoyed in movies about the 1920 and 1930s. Findings by the Special Senate Committee to Investigate Organized Crime in Interstate Commerce, headed by Senator Estes Kefauver in 1950 and the McClellan hearings in 1963-64 revealed the brutal activities of the underworld and instigated more vigorous attempts at reform and containment. Most illegal slot machines and walk-in bookie joints disappeared from sight. They still existed, of course, as did floating card and "crap" games — just less conspicuous.

LEGAL GAMBLING AGAIN
BECOMES ACCEPTABLE

Since the 1970s, the United States has turned full circle in its attitude towards gambling. Three hundred years ago, the "sport," especially in the form of lotteries, was seen as a perfectly acceptable way to raise money for public purposes. Over the past several years, slow economic growth, cuts in federal funding to states, and growing public needs have forced many desperate state and even local governments to seek additional sources of revenue. Most states have turned to lotteries, horse and dog racing, and, most recently, a growing number of states have turned to casino gambling, as a way to "painlessly" raise money for the public coffers. Indian reservations, many mired in poverty, have turned to gambling in order to replace dwindling federal funds.

While moral issues and concerns about criminal involvement usually play a part in state and local election campaigns to institute legalized gambling, they are almost always overcome by the prospect of even less attractive alternatives: decreased social programs and/or increased taxes. Increased fiscal need often overrides any moral consideration for many Americans.

5

CHAPTER II

THE UNITED STATES VS. GAMBLING

FEDERAL GAMBLING LEGISLATION

PUBLIC POLICY ON GAMBLING

Current gambling policies at the state and federal levels reflect the mixed feelings Americans have toward gambling. Over the years, Americans have generally held one of two strong, conflicting beliefs about gambling — that it is morally and socially destructive and it must be eliminated, or that its enormous popularity makes it a suitable activity for government licensing and taxation. With the nation's apparently increasing tolerance for once-prohibited activities, coupled with a growing need for state and local revenues, the lure of gambling revenues has prompted most states to reconsider their gambling policies.

TRYING TO CONTROL CRIME CROSSING STATE LINES AND BORDERS

The first modern anti-gambling legislation was passed to outlaw the use of "floating casinos." During the 1940s, gambling took place on ships off the California coast, just outside the country's three-mile limit, in order to avoid prohibitions against gambling. The federal government did not approve and in 1948, Congress passed 18 USC 1081-1083*, which effectively halted the operation of gambling ships off the coast of the United States by prohibiting transportation to and from the ships.

The Kefauver Committee (see Chapter I) investigations produced a number of statutes directed at "nation-wide crime syndicates." The Johnson Act (15 USC 1171-1177), a group of statutes produced by the Kefauver Committee, prohibited the interstate transportation of illegal gambling devices. This law supported state policies outlawing slot machines and successfully eliminated interstate traffic in coin-operated gambling machines.

Throughout the 1950s, most federal efforts to control gambling were undertaken by the Internal Revenue Service (IRS). The IRS attacked illegal gambling operations under the Wagering Excise Tax and Wagering Occupational Stamp Tax statue (26 USC 4401 and 26 USC 4411). (See page 8.)

The (John F.) Kennedy Administration (1961-1963) was committed to controlling illegal gambling. During the 1960s, Congress passed statutes that attacked large gambling syndicates operating across state lines (18 USC 1081-1804 and 18 USC 1952). With the passage of these statutes, the federal government attempted to suppress large-scale interstate gambling operations by allowing local and state governments to extend their investigations across state boundaries.

The interstate transportation of wagering paraphernalia is defined under PL 91-452 (18 USC 1952-53) and contains the broadest anti-gambling provisions: it prohibits interstate travel or the use of interstate facilities to promote illegal gambling enterprises. Statutes 18 USC 1084 and 18 USC 1952 have been most effective against interstate

---

* This and the following citations refer to the United States Code. The number preceding the USC is the volume. The number after the USC is the section.

bookmaking operations and were essential in closing down the lavish, large-scale illegal casinos that flourished in major cities during the 1940s and 1950s. Before these statutes were passed, a large interstate layoff bookmaking operation existed throughout the country (see Arnold Rothstein, Chapter I) and single layoff operations (in which a bookie turns to other bookies to help handle larger bets) supported bookmaking establishments in a number of states.

Federal law enforcement agencies were more effective in combating interstate gambling syndicates than were state or local governments because federal authorities could operate more easily across state lines and they were somewhat less susceptible to payoffs. The federal effort substantially eliminated interstate bookkeeping operations controlled by organized crime and all but the two most prevalent forms of illegal gambling — the numbers and bookmaking.

TARGETING ORGANIZED CRIME

The passage of the *Organized Crime Control Act of 1970* (PL 91-452) significantly expanded federal jurisdiction over gambling. Despite all the government's previous efforts to control syndicated gambling, Congressional hearings and research revealed that gambling was still the largest single source of income for organized crime.

Provision 18 USC 1955 of the *Organized Crime Control Act* changed the federal government's basis for attacking organized gambling. First, it defined an illegal, organized gambling operation as one that involved five or more people in the conduct, financing, directing, managing, or ownership of a gambling business doing a gross volume of $2,000 per day, or operating continually over a 30-day period, and in violation of the law in a particular state. It also broadened the federal government's control over interstate commerce by requiring only general, rather than specific, knowledge of illegal activities as cause to apprehend lawbreakers.

Recommended modifications to 18 USC 1955 include redefining an illegal gambling operation by reducing the number of operation employees from five to three and increasing the gross volume to $10,000 per day. Restrictions on prosecuting gambling business that are not controlled by organized crime have also been suggested.

Corrupt public officials often play a major role in organized crime operations. Statute 18 USC 1511 of the *Organized Crime Control Act* prohibits an elected or appointed public official from using his or her position to hinder an investigation of illegal gambling activity.

GAMBLING AND RACKETEERING

Statutes 18 USC 1961-68 provide civil remedies for gambling activities. These provisions, enacted as part of the Organized Crime Control Act of 1970, are collectively known as the RICO (Racketeer-Influenced and Corrupt Organizations) statutes. The RICO statutes permit the federal government to act in a civil or criminal case against anyone engaged in two separate acts of "racketeering activity" (obtaining money illegally). Transmitting gambling information, interstate transportation of wagering paraphernalia, and illegal gambling businesses became offenses punishable by imprisonment.

The civil remedy provision, 18 USC 1964, does not normally involve imprisonment. However, this provision permits a court to order individuals to divest themselves of interests which are in violation of RICO statutes, to impose reasonable restrictions on future activities and investments of such persons, and to order the dissolution or reorganization of such enterprises involved in racketeering activities. These long-term preventive actions, while not putting the violator in jail, can sometimes provide more practical protection from racketeering activity than would criminal punishment.

An extremely important part of statute 18 USC 1964 is that if a defendant violates a court order, he or she must show cause why he or she should not be held in contempt of court, while the government must only show that the order has been violated. This lowers the government's burden of proof and thereby allows a rapid response to any violations of the court's order. Finally, in a civil case, the government need only prove by "a preponderance of the evidence" (or the bulk of the evidence) that the defendant is likely in the future to engage in conduct that violates the law. This means that a violator can be put in prison, not because he or she has been guilty "beyond a reasonable doubt," as in normal criminal proceedings, but because "a preponderance of the evidence," shows that a court order has been violated.

The RICO statutes have had great success in stemming illegal gambling in the United States, but many civil libertarians question the use of this law which has been used as an easy way to prosecute alleged lawbreakers, ranging from those charged with pornography, to those arrested for picketing abortion clinics.

TAXABLE EARNINGS

Since the Prohibition Era (1920-1933), tax laws have been used to control organized crime. In fact, Al Capone was booked for income-tax evasion even before the investigation of his illegal bootlegging activities was completed, and he went to jail for not paying his taxes, not for his many other criminal activities. On the other hand, some tax laws have contributed to the success of illegal gambling operations and thereby promoted organized crime.

Section 61 of the Internal Revenue Service code describes as taxable income "any accretion to wealth ... unless specifically exempt," which means gambling winnings are taxable. Since most persons wager or bet for entertainment, few small winners coming home from a moderately successful trip to Las Vegas or Atlantic City are likely to declare their winnings. Few gamblers are net winners during a given year, or for that matter, during their gambling careers, but most gamblers think

that at some time they will become big winners. Winners who properly declare their gambling income are not permitted to carry back or carry forward losses from previous or later years as a deduction against their current winnings (an economic disadvantage), as they would in the case of normal earnings. Consequently, the tax laws tend to encourage patronage of illegal games. Furthermore, a big winner knows that a legal gambling establishment will report his or her winnings to the IRS, while the winner in an illegal game can safely assume that the operator will not file a report of his business activities.

Certainly one of the most controversial recommendations made by the Commission on the Review of the National Policy Toward Gambling in 1976 was to repeal taxes on gambling winnings in order to take away a major edge held by illegal gambling. Some experts believe that if taxes on gambling were repealed, it could have a significant impact in eliminating illegal gambling operations. A change in the tax policy, however, is most unlikely.

In 1951, in an attempt to raise money, Congress passed the Wagering Excise Tax (26 USC 4401) and the Wagering Occupational Stamp Tax (26 USC 441). Originally, for those engaged in gambling activities, the excise tax was 10 percent of earnings plus a $50 charge for the occupational stamp required of each person involved in gambling operations. On December 1, 1974, Congress changed these requirements to 2 percent and $500, respectively, in an effort to enable legal bookmakers who pay the taxes to compete more effectively with their illegal competitors. This wagering tax applies only to sports, horse bookmaking, and numbers games — it does not apply to pari-mutuel betting, coin-operated machines, state lotteries that base winnings on horse race results, or casino games.

Although the laws discussed here were intended to limit illegal gambling activity, little money or manpower has been devoted to their enforcement. In fact, these laws have hurt legal state-sanctioned gambling operations because legal operators are far more likely to pay taxes than illegal operators, and hence, they are unable to offer the same return on a wager as the illegal operations. Therefore, the Commission on the Review of the National Policy Toward Gambling recommended that the excise and occupational taxes be eliminated, as well as the $250 Occupational Tax on Coin-Operated Devices (26 USC 4411), passed in 1941. None of the tax recommendations made by the Commission has yet been instituted.

GAMBLING ON NATIVE AMERICAN RESERVATIONS

Because of historical tribal treaties, Native American reservations have been under exclusive federal jurisdiction and thereby exempt from the laws of the state in which they were located. However, under PL 83-280, passed in 1968, Congress granted civil and criminal jurisdiction over reservations to the states, as long as the move was approved by tribal consent. This statute was passed with the understanding that federal supervision would gradually be eliminated and state jurisdiction would prevail. The most controversial issue arising from PL 83-280 concerns taxation — it prohibits the states from collecting a tax on Indian activities. Nevertheless, many state governments, searching for additional sources of revenue, have shown an interest in collecting such taxes, but their efforts, so far, have failed.

Turning to Bingo

Like the states, Native American tribes also saw their federal funding cut back during the 1980s and they began looking for another source of income. Many tribes decided to take advantage of their unique status and have set up gambling (mainly bingo) operations on their reservations. By the end of the 1980s, Native-American tribes were sponsoring over 100 gambling operations, most of them high-stakes bingo games, which were producing more than $100 million in revenues annually for the tribes. Some bingo games had become so big that prizes reach $100,000.

Wanting a Part of the Take Trying to Tax the Income

Not surprisingly, many states in which the reservations were located wanted to regulate and, perhaps, tax the income from the gambling. The State of Florida wanted to regulate bingo games being played on Seminole land, but the Fifth Circuit Court of Appeals, in *Seminole Tribe of Florida v. Butterworth* (658 F.2d 310, 1981) ruled that the state could not regulate bingo on the reservation if the game were legal in the state. The Supreme Court denied *certiorari* (would not hear) (455 US 1020, 1982) letting the lower court decision stand. (*Barona Groups of Captain Grande Band of Mission Indians v. State of Wisconsin*, [694 F.2d 1185, 1982] and O*neida Tribe of Indians v. State of Wisconsin* [518 F. Supp. 712, 1981] produced similar rulings.)

In 1987, the U.S. Supreme Court, in *California v. Cabazon of Mission Indians*, (55 LW 4225) upheld its earlier finding, ruling that states generally may not regulate gaming on Native American reservations, but that the federal government does have the authority to regulate or forbid Native-American gaming enterprises and to delegate authority to the states.

In 1986, the Bureau of Indian Affairs (BIA) reversed a long-standing policy by notifying Indian tribes that the BIA must approve bingo management contracts with outside companies. This ruling was an attempt by the federal government to become involved in what had previously been a state-regulated gambling industry. The federal government was concerned about the possibility of organized crime controlling gambling on Native American reservations and that large gambling winnings might go unreported, since tribal revenues are unaudited and cannot be taxed.

The Indian Gaming Regulatory Act

Meanwhile, Congress had already begun to try to resolve the problem. Like many controversial issues, it took a long time (six years) to reach a compromise that would satisfy the competing factions. The federal government claimed to be concerned that organized crime would take over the Native American games, the states were offended by any gambling activities within their borders that they did not regulate, and the Native Americans resented any intrusion on their lands or tribal rights.

In 1988, Congress passed, and President Ronald Reagan signed into law, the "Indian Gaming Regulatory Act" (IGRA, PL 100-497) which permits:

> Indian tribes [to] have the exclusive right to regulate gaming activity on Indian lands if the gaming activity is not specifically prohibited by Federal law and is conducted within a State which does not, as a matter of criminal law and public policy, prohibit such gaming activity.

The law creates three different categories of gambling. "Class I gaming" refers to "social games solely for prizes of minimal value or traditional forms of Indian gaming" which would be regulated only by the tribe. "Class II gaming," which includes bingo, lotto, and other games similar to bingo (and specifically does not include baccarat, chemin de fer, or blackjack), would be under the regulation of a National Indian Gaming Commission set up by the law. "Class III gaming" refers to all other forms of gambling including casinos, slot machines and horse and dog racing. These gambling activities would not take place on the Native American lands unless they were permitted in the state and unless the tribe reached an agreement with the state.

A "grandfather clause" would permit certain card games, most notably blackjack, to be continued to be played in the states of Michigan, North Dakota, South Dakota, and Washington since they were already in operation.

The National Indian Gaming Commission was to consist of three full-time members, the Chairman appointed by the President of the United States with the advice and consent of the Senate, and the other two appointed by the Secretary of the Interior. No more than two members could come from the same political party and at least two members had to be enrolled in a Native American tribe. The Commission has the power to regulate Class II and Class III gambling on Native American lands, although Class III gambling would also be controlled by agreements between the tribe and the state within which its lands lie. Finally, the states could not tax the Native American earnings from gambling, and, in fact, the law specifically states that a court "shall consider any demand by the State for direct taxation of the Indian tribe or of any Indian lands as evidence that the State has not negotiated in good faith."

State-Tribal Compacts

As a result of the law, states and tribes have entered compacts to permit gambling facilities to be developed on Native American lands. By November 1993, 78 tribes in 18 states had reached 93 compacts with the governments in the states within which their lands were located. Many of these compacts have already led to many very successful casino operations and more will develop in the near future. (See Chapter V.)

Not Always Easy

Nonetheless, the procedure of making state compacts has not always been easy. Some states have been reluctant to negotiate with Native Americans. On the other side, many Native American leaders resent having to deal with state officials. In the past, they have only had to deal with federal officials. In addition, many Native American leaders believe that having to reach a compact agreement with states compromises their authority as sovereign nations.

Several states have gone to court in order to avoid reaching a compact with a Native American tribe claiming the Tenth Amendment, which reserves the right to the states all powers not delegated to the federal government by the Constitu-

10

tion, and the Eleventh Amendment, which indicates that a state may not be sued by individuals based on federal legislation (unless clearly so stated by Congress). The lower courts have reached mixed findings on these questions and the resolution of the issue will have to await the rulings of higher courts.

State dissatisfaction with the existing legislation exploded in Arizona in a year-long battle that finally ended with the Secretary of the Interior Bruce Babbit working out a compromise. The incident began in May 1992 with Federal Bureau of Investigation (FBI) raiding five reservations that were operating slot machines without compacts. The Fort McDowell Yavapai resisted, surrounded the governments vehicles with three dozen of their own, and faced down the federal authorities. A short-term compromise was negotiated allowing up to 250 slot machines on the reservations and the standoff ended. Later mediation followed which allowed more slot machines and the eventual development of complete casinos.

Arizona Governor Fife Symington responded by asking the state legislature to ban all forms of gambling in the state. (Later he said would rather legalized gambling in the state than give the Native Americans a monopoly.) After considerable political wrangling, both sides approached Secretary Babbit who arranged a compromise compact basing the amount of gambling equipment on the size of the tribe. Basically, the state was recognizing the reality of Native American gaming.

National Indian Gaming Commission

Finally, after several years, the National Indian Gaming Commission (NIGC) finally reached full membership and began to prepare long overdue guidelines to provide some oversight for the Native American gambling industry. Beginning in 1993, the National Indian Gaming Commission began daily oversight of Class II gaming (mainly bingo) and, with approval of management, contracts and tribal rules on Class III gaming (casinos, slot machines, etc.). Most regulation on Class III gaming, however, will be established in the state-tribe compacts.

Many tribal leaders resent NIGC having any control over them. They feel they have had two hundred years of oversight by federal agencies, most notably the Bureau of Indian Affairs, and it has done them little good. They feel they are fully capable of running their reservations and the business done on those reservations and they do not need NIGC looking over their shoulders. The tribal leaders know that certainly some of them will fail and others may be cheated by unscrupulous, business people, but these circumstances happen in all sorts of business endeavors and there is no reason they should be singled out for oversight. Nonetheless, the NIGC hopes to have the tribes eventually submit financial statements to the Commission on a regular basis.

There are approximately 300 tribes in the United States (about 200 in Alaska) and it will not be easy for the NIGC to find agreement among this large group. Like any group of hundreds of different sovereign entities, they have hundreds of different positions and needs. Just as there is no single generic nation in the world, there is no single generic Native American tribe. The NIGC will have to recognize this diversity and learn to work with this wide variety of opinions and situations.

Attempts in Congress
to Limit Native American Gambling

The rapid growth of casino gambling on Native-American reservations has led the introduction of several proposed pieces of legislation designed to change the Indian Gaming Regulatory Act (IGRA). In 1993, New Jersey Representative Robert Torricelli (D-NJ) and Nevada Senator Harry Reid (D-NV) introduced similar bills on the same day calling for the limiting of Native-American gambling. Representative Torricelli's bill, the "Gaming Integrity and State Enforcement Act of 1993," and Senator Reid's proposal, the "Indian Gaming Regulatory Act Amendments" both prohibit Native American gambling compacts unless the state permits the gaming as part of a commercial, for-profit enterprise within the state. In addition, just because a state permits one type of Class III gaming, most notably a lottery, does not mean that they have to permit other forms of Class III gaming, most likely a casino.

Both bills also propose to make the state a more equal power in the preparation of the compact and less subject to the threat that they are not bargaining in good faith. Both Congressmen claim that Native American gaming has gotten out of control. Meanwhile, Senator Daniel Inouye (D-HI), Chairman of the Senate Indian Affairs Committee, has spent a great deal of time, meeting with Native American leaders and government officials in an effort to reach a compromise that will essentially leave IGRA intact.

ADVERTISING FOR LOTTERIES

Title 18 USC Para. 1302 prohibits the mailing of any "publication of any kind containing any advertisement of any lottery, gift enterprise, or scheme of any kind offering prizes dependent in whole or in part upon lot or chance, or containing any list of the prizes drawn or awarded by means of any such lottery, gift, enterprise, or scheme." This law dated back to the 1940s when lotteries were illegal. By the 1980s, most states had a lottery and many wanted to advertise the lottery through promotions sent out directly through the mail and/or in newspapers which are often sent through the mail. The Minnesota Newspaper Association challenged the law, and a federal district court, in *Minnesota Newspaper Assn., Inc. v. Postmaster General* (677 F. Supp. 1400, 1987), ruled the law valid as it applied to advertisements, but unconstitutional as applied to prize lists since the law could prevent the publication of prize lists in news reports and that would be a violation of the freedom of the press.

The case was appealed all the way to the U.S. Supreme Court. However, before the Supreme Court could hear the case, the U.S. Congress was seeking a legislative remedy to this problem. Con-gress passed and the President signed into law the "Charity Games Advertising Clarification Act of 1988" (PL 100-625). This law indicates that the existing federal law should not apply to advertisements or radio broadcasts concerning lotteries prepared by either state or non-profit organizations which are published or broadcast in a state that conducts a lottery. The law also applies to private companies that are using a lottery as a promotional activity ("but only a promotional activity and only occasional[ly]").

Based on this new law, the Postmaster General agreed that the law no longer applied to the noncommercial publishing of prize lists. Since there was no longer any live controversy, the Supreme Court, in *Frank, Postmaster General of the United States v. Minnesota Newspaper Association, Inc.* (57 LW 4462, 1989), finding there was no longer a controversy, declared the case moot and referred it back to the lower court to be dismissed.

SPORTS GAMBLING

During the late 1980s and early 1990s, several states have tried to introduce sports betting, either as part of the lottery (similar to a sports pool) or as sports bookmaking. Attempts to introduce sports bookmaking in California, to counter the sports bookmaking operations across the Mexican-American border in Northern Baja California, Mexico, have failed as have attempts in New York, Illinois, and New Jersey.

Fear of Gambling in the Sports Industry

Nonetheless, the leaders of the nation's sports industry, including the National Basketball Association (NBA) and the National Football League (NFL), and Major League Baseball, were concerned that the states in their desperation to raise monies might begin to tie sports betting with their lotteries as had Oregon. They began to put strong pressure on state legislatures not to introduce sports betting. The sports industry also started lobbying Congress and as a result several bills have been introduced in the U.S. Congress to limit the growth of sports wagering, either as part of a lottery or as sports bookmaking. The most notable were two similar bills, one proposed by Senator Dennis DeConcini (D-AZ) (S 474) and the other by Representative John Bryant (D-TX) (HR 74).

Gambling is Bad for Sports

At hearings on HR 74, representatives from the NBA and the NFL strongly supported the bill. They believed that legal gambling on sports would threaten the integrity of their games. Any missed basketball shot or field goal that hooked away from the goal posts would be suspect. Had the player missed the shot or the kick because some gambler had paid him money? What about a terrible call by the referee? Was the game fixed? These are questions the sports leagues believe could threaten their businesses. (See Chapter IX for a discussion of public attitudes as to whether various sporting events are fixed.)

NFL Commissioner Paul Tabliabue declared that:

> We do not want our games used as bait to sell gambling. Sports gambling should not be used as a cure for the sagging fortunes of Atlantic City casinos or to boost public interest in state lotteries. We should not gamble with our children's heroes.

NBA Commissioner David Stern added that:

> Sports betting alters the interest of spectators from that of fans, who are principally interested in the ultimate outcome of the game, to that of gamblers, who are principally interested in beating the point spread and winning their bets.

Finally, some legislators believe that sports gambling could be a bad influence on young people. Senator DeConcini indicated that:

The spread of legalized sports gambling threatens to lure our youth into all types of gambling. It threatens the very foundation of professional and amateur sporting events, which is to provide wholesome entertainment for all ages.

Sports is Just Another Opportunity for Gambling

Opponents of the bills, mainly representatives from the various states which were considering such gambling possibilities in order to raise money, plus the North American Association of State & Provincial Lotteries (NASPL), believed the sports leagues were being hypocritical and wondered why the sports businesses are willing to accept sport betting in Nevada, but will not accept it in other states that need the money just as badly. Furthermore, they argued, the sports leagues were aware that billions of dollars are bet illegally on sporting events, so that the opportunity for gambler's influence on players and referees already existed.

NASPL President James Hosker observed that:

> More than $1.5 billion is wagered annually on sports in Nevada and an estimated $15 billion to $20 billion nationwide. The leagues have long been aware of this activity and have taken virtually no action to prevent it. If this has not undermined the integrity of professional sports, state-sponsored sports lotteries will not do so.

Similarly, Oregon Lottery Director James Davey observed:

> The leagues have long known of extensive wagering in Nevada and the publication of point spread in virtually every major newspaper and have done nothing. . . The leagues' attempts to ban carefully regulated, state-run sports pool lotteries cannot be justified.

Proponents further pointed out that the various pre-game sports shows (usually for football games) featured the point spreads (see Chapter VIII) that the sports leagues knew were used for betting on the games. Apparently stung by such criticism, the National Football League (NFL) has tried to pressure the networks carrying their games not to discuss the odds or point spread on these pre-game shows, although not with great success. The National Basketball Association (NBA) sued the Oregon Lottery Commission to forbid them from using the scores of basketball games as the basis of their lottery's sports lottery game. The NBA and the Commission settled out of court with the Commission agreeing not to offer betting on professional basketball games for the next five years.

The Professional and Amateur
Sports Protection Act of 1992

On October 28, 1992, Senator DeConcini's and Bryant's bills became law as the "Professional and Amateur Sports Protection Act of 1992" (PL 102-559). The law forbids betting on professional and collegiate sports including football, basketball, and baseball. The bill exempts all existing sports betting in Delaware, Nevada, Oregon, and Montana. New Jersey has until January 1, 1994 to introduce sports betting should it choose. After that date, should the state not introduce sports betting, it could not do so. Horse racing, dog racing, and jai-alai were in no way affected by this law.

GAMBLING ON CRUISE SHIPS

When ships are three miles off the coast of the United States, there generally has been no regulation over the gambling that may or may not take place on board. In 1992, Congress approved a general maritime law (PL 102-251) that included a section on gambling on cruise ships. The law permitted U.S. flag ships within the 3-mile limit to operate gambling facilities on board as long as the gambling was not the sole purpose of the cruise and that gambling was permitted only on international and interstate (between states) voyages. This law actually applied to very few cruise ships since, of the 100 plus cruise ships that dock at American ports, barely 2 percent are registered in the United States.

Any gambling that took place on ports located within a single state would be regulated by that state. "Cruises to nowhere," trips in which the ship sails out into international waters and then cruises around while the passengers gamble, would be controlled by the state from which the ship left port. Currently, only Florida does not have a law forbidding "cruises to nowhere" and a few small companies are operating out of that state.

The passage of the law led to some difficulties in California. Some cruises leaving Los Angeles stop at other California ports (Catalina and San Diego). Although, up until the passage of the new legislation, foreign ships had been operating casino games as they traveled between California ports (intrastate), Dan Lungren, attorney-general of California, decided to reconsider the situation in the light of the new legislation.

As a result, in 1992 California passed a new law (AB3769) banning gambling on both American and foreign registered ships traveling between ports in the state. The law also reemphasized the state's ban on "cruises to nowhere." Faced with a loss of gambling revenue, several cruise lines cancelled stops in Catalina and San Diego whose tourist industry lost many millions of dollars in revenue as a result. Currently, the cruise lines are fighting to have the new law reconsidered or reinterpreted in such a way that would permit the resumption of gambling on their ships when they were travelling between California ports.

HOW SHOULD THE
GAMBLING LAWS BE CHANGED?

The fundamental questions posed a decade and a half ago by the National Gambling Commission have still not been answered. The Commission asked the nation what it really wanted to do: stop organized crime by cutting into its major source of revenue, i.e., illegal gambling, or continue taxing gambling in ways that tend to drive the gambler out of legal betting parlors and into the hands of illegal bookies.

The United States is still torn between the perceived evils of gambling and its potential for raising money for social needs such as education and care for the elderly. Nonetheless, despite moral misgivings, the United States has become far more tolerant of gambling in recent years. Most states now operate lotteries and an ever growing number of states and communities are turning to some form of casino gambling to generate income.

While organized crime may currently derive much of its income from illegal drugs and the infiltration of apparently legal businesses, illegal gambling is still a major source of revenue. The federal government, however, has made no commitment to changing existing legislation in order to make illegal gambling less attractive. While the tax money undoubtedly appears attractive, the moral issue still makes any major change in gambling policy (for instance, introducing a national lottery) a politically risky undertaking.

CHAPTER III

AN OVERVIEW OF GAMBLING ACTIVITY *

SOME DEFINITIONS

As with any industry or occupation, gambling has its own vocabulary. Following are a few terms that have a specific meaning in the gambling industry.

GAMING — same as gambling.

WAGER — same as "bet," that is, the amount of money a person spends on a gambling activity.

HANDLE — the total amount of money bet by all bettors on a specific gambling event or activity.

TAKE-OUT — the percentage of the handle that is taken out by the operator of the gambling activity (the race track operator, for example) and by the state (in the form of taxes and license fees), etc.

PAY-OFF — the amount of money left over after the take-out; the amount which is distributed among the winning bettors.

TYPES OF LEGAL GAMBLING

There are five principal forms of legal gambling in the United States: bingo, lotteries, pari-mutuel betting, off-track betting, and casinos. According to PL 91-452, the term gambling includes, but is not limited to, pool-selling, bookmaking, maintaining slot machines, roulette wheels or dice tables, conducting lotteries, policy, bolita or numbers games, or selling chances to these games. Legal gambling operations can be conducted by either a state or a private enterprise. Gambling operations must follow federal statutes but are generally regulated by state governments.

In 1993, some form of legal gambling was either operating or authorized to operate in 49 states plus Washington, DC, and the jurisdictions of Puerto Rico and the U.S. Virgin Islands. The only state that had no form of legal gambling either authorized or operating was Hawaii. Bingo is the most common form of legalized gambling (45 states, Washington, DC, and Puerto Rico). Thoroughbred horse racing is permitted in 43 states (although not necessarily operating), Puerto Rico, and the Virgin Islands, and lotteries are allowed in 37 states.

Twenty-one states permit casino gambling although it has not yet been implemented in all of these states. Table 3.1 shows the types of gaming activity available throughout the United States and its jurisdictions and their operating status. Table 3.2 shows the same information for provinces and territories in Canada.

---

* The charts and much of the information in this chapter have been taken from *Gaming and Wagering Business*, the gambling industry magazine. Information Plus would like to thank *Gaming and Wagering Business* (NY) for permission to reprint this material.

A BIG BUSINESS

Gambling is big business with dramatic changes occurring over the last few years. Casino gambling, which was once limited to two states, is now legal in 21 states. At one time, only bingo parlors could be found on Native-American Reservations. Today, dozens of casinos are operating. States without lotteries are now the exception and even many southern states, such as Texas and Georgia, which were once reluctant to have lotteries, have now introduced them. As a result, horse and dog racing has generally suffered during this period of rapid change as gamblers bet their money elsewhere, although many states have permitted off-track betting to try to maintain betting on these races.

In 1992 a record $29.9 billion was earned by legal gambling companies (earnings come from the gamblers' losses), most of which came from lotteries (38 percent) and casinos (34 percent). (See Table 3.3.) This was almost three times the amount earned by gambling only 10 years before. Americans lost as much money on gambling in 1992 as they spent on jewelry and watches ($30.6 billion). They spent only a bit more on furniture for their homes ($33.4 billion) and visits to the dentist ($34.5 billion). Americans lost six times more money gambling than they spent on going to the movies or theater ($4.9 billion for admission to movies and theaters). In 1992, Americans spent .59 percent of their total personal income on legal gambling activities (Table 3.3). If the total $29.9 billion lost by gamblers in 1992 were represented as the sales revenue for one single company, that company would have been the 19th largest company in

TABLE 3.1

U.S. GAMING AT A GLANCE

	Bingo	Charitable Games	Card Rooms	Casinos	Gaming Devices	Sports Wagering	Video Lottery Terminals	Keno	Instant (& Pull-Tab) Games	Lotto	Numbers	Passives	Greyhound	Jai Alai	Harness	Quarter Horse	Thoroughbred	Interstate Inter-Track Wagering	Intrastate Inter-Track Wagering	Off-Track Betting	Telephone Betting
									Lottery Games								Parimutuel Wagering				
Alabama	•	★											•		♣	•	•	•			
Alaska	•	•																			
Arizona	•	•		★	★				•	•			•			•	•	•	•	•	
Arkansas													•		♣	•	•				
California	•	•	•					★	•	•	•	□			•	•	•	•	•	•	
Colorado	•	•	•	•	•				•	•	•	□	•				•	•	•	•	★
Connecticut	•	•		★	★				•	•	•	□	•	•	♣	♣	♣	★	•	•	
Delaware	•	•					□		•	•	•	□			•		•	•			
Florida	•	•							•	•	•		•	•	•	•	•	•		•	
Georgia	•							★	★	★											
Hawaii																					
Idaho	•								•	•			•			•	•	•	•	•	
Illinois	•	•	♣	•	•			□	•	•	•	□			•	•	•	•	•	•	
Indiana	•	•		♣	♣				•	•	•				♣	♣	♣	♣	♣	♣	
Iowa	•	•	•	•	•				•	•			•		•	•	•	•	•		
Kansas	•	•						★	•	•	★		•		□	•	•	•	•		
Kentucky	•	★							•	•	•				•	•	•	•	•	★	•
Louisiana	•	•		♣	★				•	•	★		•		□	•	•	•	•	•	
Maine	•	•							•	•	•	□			•		□	★		★	
Maryland	•	•	•		•			★	•	•	•	□			•	•	•	•	•	★	♣
Massachusetts	•	•						♣	•	•	•	□	•		•	□	•	★	★		
Michigan	•	•	•	•					•	•	•	•			•	•	•	•			
Minnesota	•	•	•	•	•				•	•	•				□	□	□	□	♣		
Mississippi	•	•		★	★																
Missouri	•	•		♣	♣				•	•	•				□	□	□	♣	♣		
Montana	•	•	•	♣	•			•	•	•					♣	•	•	•	•		
Nebraska	•	•		•					•	★	♣				•	•	•	•			
Nevada	•		•	•	•	•		•					□	□	□	•	•			•	•
New Hampshire	•	•							•	•	•	□			•		•	•			
New Jersey	•	•	★	•	•				•	•	•	□			•		•	•		★	
New Mexico	•	•													•	•	•	•			
New York	•	•		★					•	•	•	□			•	□	•	•	•		
North Carolina	•																				
North Dakota	•	•	•	•		•									•	•	•	•	♣	•	
Ohio	•	•							•	•	•	•			•	•	•	•	•	★	
Oklahoma	•	★													♣	•	•	•	•	★	
Oregon	•	•	•	•	•	•	•	★	★	•	•	•	•		•	•	•	•	•	•	
Pennsylvania	•	•							•	•	•	□			•		•	•	•		
Rhode Island	•	•					★	★	•	•	•	•	•	•	□		□	•			
South Carolina	•				•																
South Dakota	•	•	•	•	•		•		•	•			□			•	•	•	•		
Tennessee															♣	♣	♣	♣	♣		
Texas	•	•						★	★	★		★			•		•	★	★		
Utah													■								
Vermont	•	•							•	•	•	□	•				□	♣			
Virginia	•	•							•	•	•				♣	♣	♣	♣	♣	♣	
Washington	•	•	•	★				★	•	•	•				□	•	•	•	♣		
Wash., D.C.	•	•							•	•	•										
West Virginia	•	•					•	★	•	•	•	□	•		♣	•	•	•			
Wisconsin	•	•		•	•				•	•	★		•		♣	♣	•				
Wyoming	•	•													♣	•	•	•	♣	♣	
Puerto Rico	•			•	•				•	•	•				•	•	•				
Virgin Islands	•	•							♣		•					•	•				

Explanation of symbols
- • Legal and operative
- ★ Implemented since July 1991
- ♣ Authorized but not yet implemented
- □ Permitted by law and previously operative
- ■ Operative but no parimutuel wagering

Source: *International Gaming & Wagering Business*

17

the 1992 Forbes Sales 500 for the year.

GROSS WAGERS (THE HANDLE)

Americans bet almost $330 billion on legal gambling in the United States in 1992, more than two and a half times as much as the $125.7 billion bet in 1982. (See Table 3.4.) More than 3 out of 4 dollars (77 percent) were wagered at casinos, mostly in Las Vegas, NV or Atlantic City, NJ. Most of the remainder was bet on the lotteries (7 percent). (See Table 3.4.)

Over the past decade from 1982 to 1992, the amount bet in non-Nevada card rooms (places where gamblers get together and play card games for money) rose 743 percent, while the amount wagered on lotteries increased almost five-fold (496 percent). The amount bet on legal bookmaking (where the gambler bets on sporting events or horseraces) rose 292 percent over the same period. Gambling at the slot machines in Nevada and New Jersey rose 557 percent over this period, although the wagering at the tables at these two gambling centers rose only 64 percent. (See Figure 3.1.) Gambling on riverboats, unknown a decade ago, grew seven-fold in one year between 1991 and 1992. Gambling on Native American reservations, which hardly existed in 1982, and was estimated at $1.3 billion in 1990, soared more than ten-fold to an estimated $15.2 billion in 1992. (See Table 3.4.)

On the other hand, the amount of pari-mutuel wagering (betting on horses, greyhounds, and jai-alai) rose only 2 percent. In 1982, parimutuel betting had accounted for about 12 percent of all money wagered; by 1993, it accounted for only 5 percent. Betting on the horses at the racetrack fell 5 percent and wagering on jai-alai, a game in which the players hurl a small ball against the walls of the court using a curved basket attached to their arm, tumbled 32 percent. Greyhound racing barely held its own with 47 percent growth over this period. The development of off-track betting (OTB) on horseracing with a 168 percent increase over this period provided most of the growth to the struggling parimutuel industry. Most experts agree that parimutuel wagering has been the most affected by the expansion of lotteries and casino gambling. Wagering on bingo seems to have levelled off with an increase of only 44 percent from 1982 to 1990. (See Table 3.4 and Figure 3.1.)

GROSS REVENUES (THE TAKE)

Not surprisingly, the gross revenues (the amount the house keeps) rose (or fell) right along with the increase (or decrease) of the total wagering. As shown in Table 3.4, total gross wagering for most forms of gambling increased from 1982 through 1992, so it should not be surprising that

TABLE 3.2
CANADIAN GAMING AT A GLANCE

	Bingo	Charitable Games	Card Rooms	Casinos	Gaming Devices	Sports Wagering	Lottery Games Video Lottery Terminals	Keno	Instant (& Pull-Tab) Games	Lotto	Numbers	Passives	Greyhound	Jai Alai	Parimutuel Wagering Harness	Quarter Horse	Thoroughbred	Interstate Inter-Track Wagering	Intrastate Inter-Track Wagering	Off-Track Betting	Telephone Betting
Alberta	●	●		●	●	●	●		●	●	●	●			●	●	●	★		★	●
British Columbia	●	●		●	●	●			●	●	●	●			●	●	●	★	●	◆	●
Manitoba	●	●		●	●	●	●		●	●	●	●			●	●	●	●	●	●	●
New Brunswick	●				□	●	●		●	●	●	●			●	◆	●	◆	●	★	◆
Newfoundland	●	●	●		□	●	●		●	●	●	●			□	◆	□	◆	●		◆
Northwest Terr.	●	●	●			●			●	●	●	●			◆	◆	◆	◆		◆	◆
Nova Scotia	●	●			□	●	●		●	●	●	●			●	□	◆	◆	●	★	◆
Ontario	●	●		◆	◆	★			●	●	●	●			●	●	●	★	●	★	□
Prince Edward Is.	●	●			□		●		●	●	●	●			●	◆	●				◆
Quebec	●			◆	◆	●			●	●	●	●			●	◆	□	◆		◆	◆
Saskatchewan		●		●	●	●	★		●	●	●	●			●	●	●	●	●	★	◆
Yukon Terr.	●			●	●	●			●	●	●	●			◆	◆	◆	◆	◆	◆	◆

Explanation of symbols
- ● Legal and operative
- ★ Implemented since July 1991
- ◆ Authorized but not yet implemented
- □ Permitted by law and previously operative
- ■ Operative but no parimutuel wagering

Source: *International Gaming & Wagering Business*

18

TABLE 3.3

Commercial Gambling and the U.S. Economy: 1982 – 1992

	1982 Gross Revenues (Consumer Spending)	1982 Gross Revenues as a % of Personal Income	1992 Gross Revenues (Consumer Spending)	1992 Gross Revenues as a % of Personal Income	Gross Revenues as a % of Personal Income Increase (Decrease) 1982 - 1992
Pari-Mutuels					
Horses					
Tracks	$1,850,000,000	0.0693%	$1,939,309,121	0.0383%	-0.0309%
OTB	400,000,000	0.0150%	969,562,063	0.0192%	0.0042%
Total	2,250,000,000	0.0842%	2,908,871,184	0.0575%	-0.0267%
Greyhounds					
Tracks	430,000,000	0.0161%	675,367,175	0.0134%	-0.0027%
OTB			12,711,225	0.0003%	0.0003%
Total	430,000,000	0.0161%	688,078,400	0.0136%	-0.0025%
Jai Alai	112,000,000	0.0042%	89,264,492	0.0018%	-0.0024%
Total Pari-Mutuels	2,792,000,000	0.1045%	3,686,214,076	0.0729%	-0.0317%
Lotteries					
Video Lotteries			242,230,000	0.0048%	0.0048%
Other Games	2,170,000,000	0.0812%	11,214,733,000	0.2217%	0.1405%
Total Lotteries	2,170,000,000	0.0812%	11,456,963,000	0.2265%	0.1453%
Casinos					
Nevada/NJ Slots	2,000,000,000	0.0749%	5,830,586,443	0.1153%	0.0404%
Nevada/NJ Tables	2,200,000,000	0.0824%	3,120,137,399	0.0617%	-0.0207%
Cruise Ships			305,431,350	0.0060%	0.0060%
Riverboats			418,021,561	0.0083%	0.0083%
Other Commercial			224,300,143	0.0044%	0.0044%
Non-Casino Devices			242,172,466	0.0048%	0.0048%
Total Casinos	4,200,000,000	0.1573%	10,140,649,362	0.2005%	0.0432%
Legal Bookmaking					
Sports Books	7,724,862	0.0003%	50,602,000	0.0010%	0.0007%
Horse Books	18,037,685	0.0007%	46,799,000	0.0009%	0.0002%
Total Bookmaking	25,762,547	0.0010%	97,401,000	0.0019%	0.0010%
Card Rooms	50,000,000	0.0019%	660,811,000	0.0131%	0.0112%
Bingo	780,000,000	0.0292%	1,090,944,000	0.0216%	-0.0076%
Charitable Games	396,000,000	0.0148%	1,298,949,000	0.0257%	0.0109%
Indian Reservations					
Class II			429,000,000	0.0085%	0.0085%
Class III			1,069,940,000	0.0212%	0.0212%
Total Indian Reservations			1,498,940,000	0.0296%	0.0296%
Grand Total	$10,413,762,547	0.3899%	$29,930,871,438	0.5917%	0.2018%

Note: Columns may not add to totals due to rounding.

Source: Eugene Martin Christiansen in *International Gaming & Wagering Business,* August 15, 1993-September 14, 1993.

gross revenues also rose. Gross revenues almost tripled over this period, increasing from $10.4 billion in 1982 to almost $30 billion in 1992.

From 1982 through 1992, non-Nevada card rooms (up 1222 percent), legal bookmaking (up 278 percent), and lotteries (up 428 percent) showed the greatest increases. Non-bingo charitable games (up 228 percent) and slot machines and other type of gambling machines (up 192 percent) also saw large growth. Gambling on Indian Reservations, which earned virtually no money in 1982, brought in an estimated $1.5 billion in 1992. Similarly, riverboats and other commercial casinos such as

TABLE 3.4
Trends in Gross Wagering, 1982 – 1992

	Gross Wagering (Handle) 1982	Gross Wagering (Handle) 1991	Gross Wagering (Handle) 1992	1982 - 1992 Gross Wagering Increase/(Decrease) Dollars	Percent
		(Revised)			
Pari-Mutuels					
Horses					
Tracks	$9,990,628,572	$9,863,556,679 *	$9,533,550,092	($457,078,480)	-4.58%
OTB	1,707,271,903	4,028,593,038 *	4,577,705,686	2,870,433,783	168.13%
Total	11,697,900,475	13,892,149,717	14,111,255,778	2,413,355,303	20.63%
Greyhounds					
Tracks	2,208,551,898	3,463,487,796 *	3,242,150,854	1,033,598,956	46.80%
OTB		38,898,771 *	62,229,466	62,229,466	N/A
Total	2,208,551,898	3,502,386,567	3,304,380,320	1,095,828,422	49.62%
Jai Alai	622,782,363	488,368,157	425,890,129	(196,892,234)	-31.61%
Total Pari-Mutuels	14,529,234,736	17,882,904,441	17,841,526,227	3,312,291,491	22.80%
Lotteries					
Video Lotteries		354,842,000 *	1,326,353,000	1,326,353,000	N/A
Other Games		20,578,640,000 *	23,035,474,000	18,947,174,000	463.45%
Total Lotteries	4,088,300,000	20,933,482,000	24,361,827,000	20,273,527,000	495.89%
Casinos					
Nevada/NJ Slots	14,400,000,000	84,398,462,227	94,557,329,008	80,157,329,008	556.65%
Nevada/NJ Tables	87,000,000,000	149,744,002,493	143,100,618,577	56,100,618,577	64.48%
Cruise Ships		4,076,675,000	4,280,508,750	4,280,508,750	N/A
Riverboats		1,099,431,451	7,319,681,498	7,319,681,498	N/A
Other Commercial		771,022,759	3,078,234,749	3,078,234,749	N/A
Non-Casino Devices		363,503,125	557,447,916	557,447,916	N/A
Total Casinos	101,400,000,000	240,453,097,055	252,893,820,498	151,493,820,498	149.40%
Legal Bookmaking					
Sports Books	415,161,891	1,871,063,086	1,800,782,918	1,385,621,027	333.75%
Horse Books	122,809,048	392,124,903	307,512,279	184,703,231	150.40%
Total Bookmaking	537,970,939	2,263,187,989	2,108,295,197	1,570,324,258	291.90%
Card Rooms	1,000,000,000	8,399,639,000	8,428,085,000	7,428,085,000	742.81%
Bingo	3,000,000,000	4,230,164,000 *	4,306,214,000	1,306,214,000	43.54%
Charitable Games	1,200,000,000	4,605,898,000 *	4,774,841,000	3,574,841,000	297.90%
Indian Reservations					
Class II		1,397,500,000	1,430,000,000	1,430,000,000	N/A
Class III		4,038,250,000	13,744,500,000	13,744,500,000	N/A
Total Indian Reservations		5,435,750,000	15,174,500,000	15,174,500,000	N/A
Grand Total	$125,755,505,675	$304,204,122,485	$329,889,108,922	$204,133,603,247	162.33%

Notes:
* Indicates revised figures for 1991
Lottery handles for 1982 are for the twelve months ending June 30th.
Columns may not add to totals due to rounding.
(1) Average annual rate from 1983 to 1992.
(2) Average annual rate from 1985 to 1992.

Source: Eugene Martin Christiansen in *International Gaming & Wagering Business*, July 15, 1993-August 14, 1993

---

those in Colorado, which did not exist in 1982, brought in $418 million and $224 million in 1992, respectively.

At the same time, reflecting betting trends indicated earlier, not all forms of gambling showed such vigorous growth. Revenues from pari-mutuel betting increased barely 32 percent over this period, while jai-alai revenues actually dropped 20 percent. The popularity of bingo (up only 40 percent) seems to have levelled off. (See Table 3.5)

How Much Does the House Keep?

Of the $330 billion wagered in 1992, the United States gambling industry kept nearly $30 billion in gross revenues, or about 9 percent of the amount bet. Nevada/New Jersey table games and slot machines and card rooms throughout the country kept less than 8 percent of the amount bet, while lotteries retained almost half of all the money bet. Operators of bingo, charitable games (usually casino type games), and gaming played on Native American Reservations kept over one-fourth of the amount bet. (See Table 3.6.)

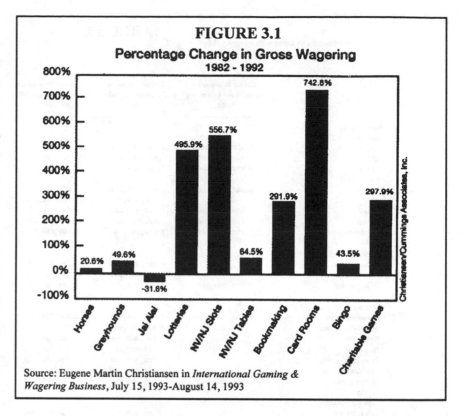

FIGURE 3.1
Percentage Change in Gross Wagering
1982 - 1992

Source: Eugene Martin Christiansen in *International Gaming & Wagering Business*, July 15, 1993-August 14, 1993

SHARE OF THE GAMBLING MARKET

Lotteries took in the largest market share (38 percent) of gross revenues, followed closely by total casino with 34 percent of the market, most of which came from the slot machines and casino tables of Las Vegas and Atlantic City. Total parimutuel betting on horses, greyhounds, and jai-alai brought in about 1 of every 8 gambling dollars (12 percent), while charitable games (4 percent) and bingo (4 percent) accounted for most of the rest. Gambling on Native American Reservations brought in about 5 percent, most of which came from newly-built casinos. (See Table 3.7.)

ILLEGAL GAMBLING

Gaming and Wagering Business, the bimonthly magazine which covers the gambling industry and the data source for much of this chapter, no longer includes illegal gambling when it counts gambling revenues. Eugene M. Christiansen, who prepares *Gaming and Wagering Business'* annual review of gaming, has noted that there is not enough reliable data to make an estimate. (See Chapter VIII for a further discussion of estimates of illegal gambling.) In 1989, *Gaming and Wagering Business* estimated that Americans lost about $6.7 billion at illegal gambling, about 22 percent of all gambling losses.

GAMBLING ON NATIVE AMERICAN RESERVATIONS

As discussed in Chapter II, the Indian Gaming Regulatory Act (PL 100-497) permits Native-American tribes to introduce gambling on their reservations. Many tribes had already been holding bingo games on their reservations, but the new law opened up the possibility that other forms of gambling could be played on Native-American lands. It also meant that the Native-American tribes would play a major role in the large expansion of gambling that was occurring throughout the country.

While returns from bingo, the major form of gambling that was being played on reservations, were beginning to level off, many Native-American tribes recognized that casino games were being offered in more places throughout the United States. (See Chapter V.) They saw this as an op-

21

TABLE 3.5

Trends in Gross Revenues, 1982 – 1992

	Gross Revenues (Consumer Spending) 1982	Gross Revenues (Consumer Spending) 1991	Gross Revenues (Consumer Spending) 1992	1982 – 1992 Gross Revenues Increase/(Decrease) Dollars	Percent	Average Annual Rate 1982-92
		(Revised)				
Pari-Mutuels						
Horses						
Tracks	$1,850,000,000	$1,990,941,596 *	$1,939,309,121	$89,309,121	4.83%	0.47%
OTB	400,000,000	859,377,651 *	969,562,063	569,562,063	142.39%	9.26%
Total	2,250,000,000	2,850,319,247	2,908,871,184	658,871,184	29.28%	2.60%
Greyhounds						
Tracks	430,000,000	711,931,075 *	675,367,175	245,367,175	57.06%	4.62%
OTB		7,565,150 *	12,711,225	12,711,225	N/A	36.56%(1)
Total	430,000,000	719,496,225	688,078,400	258,078,400	60.02%	4.81%
Jai Alai	112,000,000	100,343,331	89,264,492	(22,735,508)	-20.30%	-2.24%
Total Pari-Mutuels	2,792,000,000	3,670,158,803	3,686,214,076	894,214,076	32.03%	2.82%
Lotteries						
Video Lotteries		121,842,000	242,230,000	242,230,000	N/A	N/A
All Other Games		10,103,615,000 *	11,214,733,000	11,214,733,000	516.81%	17.85%
Total Lotteries	2,170,000,000	10,225,457,000	11,456,963,000	9,286,963,000	427.97%	18.10%
Casinos						
Nevada/NJ Slots	2,000,000,000	5,242,299,000	5,830,586,443	3,830,586,443	191.53%	11.29%
Nevada/NJ Tables	2,200,000,000	3,200,968,000	3,120,137,399	920,137,399	41.82%	3.56%
Cruise Ships		290,887,000	305,431,350	305,431,350	N/A	N/A
Riverboats		79,685,780	418,021,561	418,021,561	N/A	N/A
Other Commercial		63,912,237	224,300,143	224,300,143	N/A	N/A
Non-Casino Devices		157,680,407	242,172,466	242,172,466	N/A	N/A
Total Casinos	4,200,000,000	9,035,432,424	10,140,649,362	5,940,649,362	141.44%	9.21%
Legal Bookmaking						
Sports Books	7,724,862	52,300,000	50,602,000	42,877,138	555.05%	20.68%
Horse Books	18,037,685	55,079,878	46,799,000	28,761,315	159.45%	10.00%
Total Bookmaking	25,762,547	107,379,878	97,401,000	71,638,453	278.07%	14.22%
Card Rooms	50,000,000	659,114,000	660,811,000	610,811,000	1221.62%	29.45%
Bingo	780,000,000	1,067,753,000 *	1,090,944,000	310,944,000	39.86%	3.41%
Charitable Games	396,000,000	1,243,343,000 *	1,298,949,000	902,949,000	228.02%	12.61%
Indian Reservations						
Class II		419,250,000	429,000,000	429,000,000	N/A	25.50%(2)
Class III		300,900,000	1,069,940,000	1,069,940,000	N/A	N/A
Total Indian Reservations		720,150,000	1,498,940,000	1,498,940,000	N/A	N/A
Grand Total	$10,413,762,547	$26,728,786,105	$29,930,871,438	$19,517,108,891	187.42%	11.14%

Notes:
* Indicates revised figures for 1991
Lottery revenues for 1982 are for the twelve months ending June 30th.
Columns may not add to totals due to rounding.
(1) Average rate calculated from 1984 to 1992.
(2) Average rate calculated from 1985 to 1992.

Source: Eugene Martin Christiansen in *International Gaming & Wagering Business*, August 15, 1993-September 14, 1993.

portunity to bring some prosperity to their reservations.

The Indian Gaming Regulatory Act permitted the tribes to conduct any type of gambling on their reservation which was permitted in the state within which the reservation was located. The law also called for the tribe and the state to negotiate agreements or "compacts" which would allow this gambling. These compacts would enable types of gambling to take place on reservations that were not permitted in the state. The state was required to bargain with the tribes in good faith. If they did not, or if the tribe was not satisfied with the process, the law permitted the tribe to take the issue to court, an option Native Americans have frequently used. By 1993, according to the Bureau of Indian Affairs, 62 tribes in 18 states had negotiated compacts which permit casino gambling, a trend likely to increase.

The amount of money bet on Native-American reservations has risen from nothing in 1982 to an estimated $15 billion in 1992. The reservation retains about 10 percent of the handle, giving the tribes an estimated $1.5 billion in 1992. Of this amount, about $1.1 billion came from casino gambling and about $400 million came from bingo. Gambling revenue from reservations has been increasing rapidly with income more than doubling from 1991 alone. In all likelihood, these numbers will continue to increase dramatically. (See Chapter V for a more complete discussion of gambling on Native-American reservations.)

SPORTS GAMBLING

Sports gambling is legal and operating in four states: Montana, Nevada, North Dakota, and Oregon, and is legal, but not operative, in two states: Delaware and Indiana. Private bookmaking is legal statewide only in Nevada, while it takes places in limited localities in Montana and North Dakota and is used in Oregon as part of their lottery program. Sports betting is also legal in a number of locations in Baja California, Mexico, which borders California. The overwhelming majority of bettors visiting these border locations are Americans, mainly Californians who cross the border. (For illegal sports betting, see Chapter VIII.)

Almost all the money wagered legally on sports books is bet in Nevada. In 1992, $1.8 billion was wagered on sports in Nevada with about $50.6 million retained by the house. This is a retained percentage of only 2.8 percent. The amount and percentage of money earned by the Nevada casinos on sports betting is extremely small and the casinos generally do not consider sports betting an important source of revenue. It is also a riskier form of gambling for the house because, with a retained amount of less than 3 percent, a day in which the bettors get lucky could cost the house any profit. (See Chapter II for recent legislation on sports gambling.)

Sportbook production improved in 1993 to a handle of $1.89 billion, revenue of $64.4 million and the retained percentage increased to 3.4 per-

TABLE 3.6

1992 Gross Gambling Revenues by Industry

	% Retained	1992 Gross Revenues (Expenditures)
Pari-Mutuels		
Horses		
Tracks	20.34%	$1,939,309,121
OTB	21.18%	969,562,063
Total	20.61%	2,908,871,184
Greyhounds		
Tracks	20.83%	675,367,175
OTB	20.43%	12,711,225
Total	20.82%	688,078,400
Jai Alai	20.96%	89,264,492
Total Pari-Mutuels	20.66%	3,686,214,076
Lotteries		
Video Lotteries	18.26%	242,230,000
All Other Games	48.68%	11,214,733,000
Total Lotteries	47.03%	11,456,963,000
Casinos		
Nevada/NJ Slot Machines	6.17%	5,830,586,443
Nevada/NJ Table Games	2.18%	3,120,137,399
Cruise Ships	7.14%	305,431,350
Riverboats	5.71%	418,021,561
Other Commercial	7.29%	224,300,143
Non-Casino Devices	43.44%	242,172,466
Total Casinos	4.01%	10,140,649,362
Legal Bookmaking		
Sports Books	2.81%	50,602,000
Horse Books	15.22%	46,799,000
Total Bookmaking	4.62%	97,401,000
Card Rooms	7.84%	660,811,000
Bingo	25.33%	1,090,944,000
Charitable Games	27.20%	1,298,949,000
Indian Reservations		
Class II	30.00%	429,000,000
Class III	7.78%	1,069,940,000
Total Indian Reservations	9.88%	1,498,940,000
Grand Total	9.07%	$29,930,871,438

Note: Column may not add to totals due to rounding.

Source: Eugene Martin Christiansen in *International Gaming & Wagering Business*, August 15, 1993-September 14, 1993.

cent. Most of the money was bet on football (40.27 percent), basketball (29.43 percent), and baseball (23.48 percent).

COMPULSIVE GAMBLERS

As can be concluded from the many surveys taken on gambling, for most people who bet, gambling is a form of recreation and fun. (See Chapter IX.) While they receive enjoyment from the game, they can take or leave it. Even when they lose, they usually look upon it as the cost of entertainment and it does not upset them.

TABLE 3.7

Market Shares (Revenues), 1992 and Change from 1991

	1991 Gross Revenues (Expenditures) Market Shares	1992 Gross Revenues (Expenditures) Market Shares	Market Share Increase (Decrease)
Total Lotteries	38.26%	38.28%	0.02%
All Other Lottery Games	37.80%	37.47%	-0.33%
Total Casinos	33.80%	33.88%	0.08%
Nevada/NJ Slot Machines	19.61%	19.48%	-0.13%
Total Pari-Mutuels	13.73%	12.32%	-1.42%
Nevada/NJ Table Games	11.98%	10.42%	-1.55%
Total Horse Racing	10.66%	9.72%	-0.95%
Horse Tracks	7.45%	6.48%	-0.97%
Total Indian Reservations	2.69%	5.01%	2.31%
Charitable Games	4.65%	4.34%	-0.31%
Bingo	3.99%	3.64%	-0.35%
Class III Indian	1.13%	3.57%	2.45%
Horse OTB	3.22%	3.24%	0.02%
Total Greyhound Racing	2.69%	2.30%	-0.39%
Greyhound Tracks	2.66%	2.26%	-0.41%
Card Rooms	2.47%	2.21%	-0.26%
Class II Indian	1.57%	1.43%	-0.14%
Riverboats	0.30%	1.40%	1.10%
Cruise Ships	1.09%	1.02%	-0.07%
Video Lotteries	0.46%	0.81%	0.35%
Non-Casino Devices	0.59%	0.81%	0.22%
Other Commercial Casinos	0.24%	0.75%	0.51%
Total Bookmaking	0.40%	0.33%	-0.08%
Jai Alai	0.38%	0.30%	-0.08%
Sports Books	0.20%	0.17%	-0.03%
Horse Books	0.21%	0.16%	-0.05%
Greyhound OTB	0.03%	0.04%	0.01%

Source: Eugene Martin Christiansen in *International Gaming & Wagering Business,* August 15, 1993-September 14, 1993

For some people, however, gambling is a compulsion, a disease they cannot control. These people may become addicted to gambling and, like alcoholism, it may take control of their behavior and destroy their lives. The addiction may cause them to gamble away their paychecks or get deep into debt. It may threaten their marriages and their relationships with their children, relatives, and friends.

Characteristics of Compulsive Gamblers

The Council on Compulsive Gambling of New Jersey, Inc. "aims to reduce and prevent this insidious disease by mobilizing public support through public information and education and through interaction with professional groups concerned with the growing impact of pathological gambling." The agency offers a toll-free line, 1-800-GAMBLER to provide help to compulsive gamblers.

Arnie Wexler, Executive Director of the Council on Compulsive Gambling of New Jersey, Inc., annually surveys callers to the agency hotline. In 1992, 22,640 people called the 1-800-GAMBLER number, twice as many as the 11,069 who called in 1991. Eighty percent were male and 20 percent were female. The proportion of females calling has increased sharply from 13 percent in 1990. The average caller had 2.4 children.

Those responding to the survey bet on a wide variety of games — 73 percent played casino games, 47 percent wagered on sporting events, 52 percent bought lottery tickets, 38 percent played the horses, 3 percent bet on bingo, and 3 percent bought stocks and commodities. The typical caller was $34,244 in debt with an average annual income of $36,944. Off all the calls received, 65 percent were made by the gamblers and 35 percent were from another person who were seeking help for the gambler or for members of the gambler's family.

In a 1989 survey of 196 obsessive gamblers who had called the hotline, Wexler found that the gamblers were generally not happy with their situation. Seventy-eight percent had been bailed out (had their gambling debts paid off by somebody). However, after having been bailed out, 91 percent continued to gamble. About 69 percent of the respondents said they had thoughts of suicide and 17 percent claimed to have actually tried to kill themselves. Three-fourths (75 percent) had committed a felony because of their compulsive gambling — 35 percent stole for money, 18 percent embezzled money, and 22 percent wrote bad checks.

About one-fourth (24 percent) also had another addiction. Nine percent were alcoholics, 3 percent used drugs, 6 percent were smokers, and 11 percent were overeaters. Some were combinations of all these addictions. Of this group, Wexler found that 68 percent were going for some type of help for their addictions.

GAMBLERS ANONYMOUS

Gamblers Anonymous offers a 12-step program similar to Alcoholics Anonymous. Currently, an estimated 12,000 people attend Gamblers Anonymous meetings at about 800 locations across the nation. All members share two goals - to stop themselves from gambling and to help other compulsive gamblers to do the same. Gamblers Anonymous can be reached by calling (213) 386-8789 or writing Gamblers Anonymous, International Service Office, P.O. Box 17173, Los Angeles, CA 90017. They will supply anyone who requests with the location of the nearest Gamblers Anonymous location. All information is kept confidential — no one will know.

COMPULSIVE GAMBLING CENTER

The Compulsive Gambling Center, Inc., 924 East Baltimore St., Baltimore, MD 21202-4739 is a not-for-profit residential and outpatient treatment center. The organization offers a toll-free line (1-800-332-0402) which a compulsive gambler may call for help.

CHAPTER IV

PARI-MUTUEL BETTING — HORSES, DOGS, AND JAI-ALAI*

HOW PARI-MUTUEL BETTING WORKS

The term "pari-mutuel" describes a method of betting in which the persons who pick the winners in a given event divide the total amount of money bet in proportion to their wagers. Winnings, or payoffs, are paid on the win (first place), place (second place), and show (third place) categories of a given event, or on certain combinations of these categories.

The amount of the payoff depends on the total amount wagered on a given race or game. If the winners were heavily favored, the payoff per individual is much smaller than if the winners had little money wagered or "riding" on them. For example, if a horse is a 5-to-1 favorite, it means that for every dollar bet on that horse, $5 has been bet on the other entries. If the horse has negative odds, or is an "odds-on" favorite, let us say 1 to 2, it means that for every two dollars bet on that horse, one dollar was bet on all the other horses in the race. Bettors are constantly informed of the changing odds in an event (as people place their bets) by computerized totalisator machines, which flash new betting totals and odds on the "tote board" every 60 to 90 seconds.

The minimum amount for a pari-mutuel wager is $2, but the bettor may wager any additional amount in denominations of $5, $10, $50, or $100. Of the total amount wagered on a particular race, approximately 82 to 85 percent is returned to winning bettors in the form of payoffs. Before the winning bettors collect their money, a percentage of the total amount of money bet is taken by the agency conducting the betting operation, for example, the race track operator, and by the state, in the form of taxes.

In most states where pari-mutuel gambling is legal, a person must be 18 years old to wager at a racetrack, although in Illinois a 17-year-old may bet. In Macon County, Alabama, Nebraska, and Wyoming the age is 19 years, while in Birmingham, Alabama, New York State, and Texas the le-

---

* This chapter is based upon four sources, the annual reports on gambling prepared by Eugene Martin Christiansen and presented in *Gaming & Wagering Business*, the annual *Pari-Mutuel Racing* prepared by the Association of Racing Commissioners International, Inc., and the annual *Summary of State Pari-Mutuel Tax Structures* and *Annual Report* prepared by the American Greyhound Track Operators Association. Christiansen's study is the best generally-available overview of gambling in the United States and his information is most current. *Pari-Mutuel Racing* is more detailed, but the latest release is for 1990. *Pari-Mutuel Racing* has been used for the detailed presentation on horse racing and jai-alai. The *Summary of State Pari-Mutuel Tax Structures* and the *Annual Report* provided the basis for the presentation on greyhound tracks. The overview section is based upon Christiansen's current statistics while the more detailed presentation that follows in the remainder of the chapter is based on the 1990 statistics found in *Pari-Mutuel Racing*.

gal age for wagering is 21 years. However, most states do not have an age restriction on simply attending an event, although several do require that a minor be accompanied by an adult.

HISTORY OF THE PARI-MUTUEL SYSTEM

Pari-mutuel betting, the standard form of wagering on horses, was invented by a Frenchman in 1865. This new method of wagering made its first American appearance in 1871 at New York's Jerome Park and became an established feature of horse racing when it was successfully used at the 1908 Kentucky Derby.

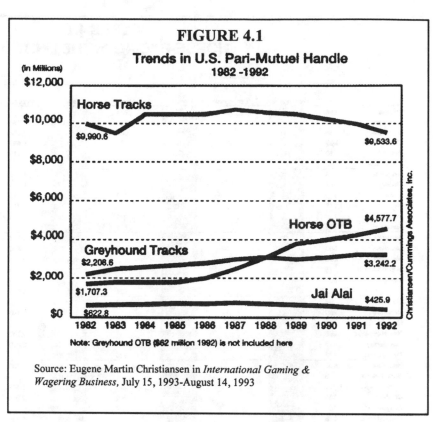

FIGURE 4.1

Trends in U.S. Pari-Mutuel Handle
1982 -1992

Source: Eugene Martin Christiansen in *International Gaming & Wagering Business*, July 15, 1993-August 14, 1993

Before pari-mutuel wagering was introduced, the race track bookmaker was a dominant figure. The bookmaker was an agent, or professional bettor, against whom the layman (non-professional) bettor wagered his own expertise and hunches. As a competitor to the layman, the bookie held a clear advantage. With the invention of pari-mutuel wagering, the bookie's position was weakened because the pari-mutuel system allowed the bettor to wager against his peers, instead of against professional bookmakers. This system also increased the bettor's return on his investment by allowing him to receive payoffs on second and third place finishes.

PARI-MUTUEL BETTING TODAY

Pari-mutual wagering is the most common form of betting on horse races (thoroughbred, harness, and quarter horse), dog races, and jai-alai games. Most pari-mutuel betting is done at the race track or game site where the event is actually taking place, but in many states, bettors can also place pari-mutuel bets at off-track and simulcast sites (see Chapter VII) and via telephone.

Pari-mutuel wagering is legal in all but six states (Alaska, Georgia, Hawaii, Mississippi, North Carolina, and South Carolina) and Washington, D.C. In 1992, the gross wagering handle on all pari-mutuel events was almost $17.8 billion.

AN OVERVIEW

The pari-mutuel industry has been hard hit by many of the recent changes in the gambling industry. The huge growth of lotteries over the past decade has given gamblers another place to spend their money. Even more serious has been the recent development of casino gambling on riverboats, selected counties in a few states, and on Native-American Reservations. The nation's bettors have been provided with another option. Racetracks in Minnesota, Wisconsin, and Connecticut, where Native-American casinos have been most successful, have been badly hurt.

As shown in Figure 4.1, horse tracks have been barely holding their own over the past decade with the handle in 1992 ($9.5 billion) less than the handle a decade earlier in 1982 ($10 billion). With-

TABLE 4.1
HORSE RACING IN THE UNITED STATES

	LIVE RACING DAYS					LIVE RACES RUN				
	Total	Thoroughbred	Qtr. Horse	Harness	Mixed	Total	Thoroughbred	Qtr. Horse	Harness	Mixed
Arizona	254				254	3,185				3,185
Arkansas	65	65				638	638			
Birmingham, AL	168	112			56	1,364	1,252	112		
California	959	489	158	175	137	10,006	4,483	1,891	1,938	1,694
Colorado	10	10				115	115			
Connecticut										
Delaware	274	150		124		2,978	1,490		1,488	
Florida	557	403		154		5,878	4,030		1,848	
Idaho	113				113	1,184	513	470		201
Illinois	1,111	489		622		11,719	4,714		7,005	
Iowa	138			44	94	1,380			440	940
Kansas	114				114	1,192				1,192
Kentucky	582	285	41	256		5,667	2,738	369	2,560	
Louisiana	685	480	92		113	6,850	4,800	920		1,130
Maryland	583	277		306		6,378	2,854		3,524	
Massachusetts	19	19				190	190			
Michigan	906	181		679	46	8,890	1,906		6,532	452
Minnesota	122	88			34	1,176	1,065	111		
Montana	98				98	980				980
Nebraska	250	223	27			2,422	2,198	224		
Nevada	14				14	148				148
New Hampshire	266	256		10		2,869	2,752		117	
New Jersey	850	337		513		8,163	3,033		5,130	
New Mexico	430				430	5,305				5,305
New York	1,658	473		1,185		17,765	4,730		13,035	
North Dakota	8		4		4	85			40	45
Ohio	1,302	610	5	476	211	9,250	6,100	50	990	2,110
Oklahoma	365	119			246	3,964	2,043	1,659		262
Oregon	157				157	1,706				1,706
Pennsylvania	816	450		366		9,070	4,330		4,740	
South Dakota	15				15	174				174
Texas	113				113	1,179				1,179
Vermont	10			10		111			111	
Washington	281	212			69	2,819	2,619			200
West Virginia	474	474				4,792	4,792			
Wyoming	74				74	825				825
Totals	13,841	6,201	323	4,925	2,392	140,417	63,385	5,808	49,496	21,728

Source: *Pari-Mutuel Racing, 1990*, Association of Racing Commissioners International, Inc., Lexington, KY

out off-track-betting (OTB)* which brought in $4.6 billion in 1992, many horse tracks would be unable to make it. (For more complete statistics, see Table 3.4.)

Greyhound racing may be in an even more difficult situation. The handle at greyhound tracks dropped over 6 percent from 1991 to 1992 alone, falling from $3.5 billion to $3.2 billion. Unlike the horse tracks, dog tracks do not have the developed simulcasting systems** that is needed for OTB to be successful to make up for the fall in wagering at the track. (The total handle for OTB on greyhound racing was only $62 million in

---

* Off-track betting (OTB) means exactly what it says — a person places a bet on a horse or dog race at some location other than the track where the race actually takes place. Off-track bets are usually placed at a track branch office or a betting shop. Some states permit a bettor to call in his or her bet over the telephone. OTB operations are run by highly regulated and carefully supervised private (non-government) corporations. Revenues are distributed to state and local governments and the racing industry (which includes the OTB corporations themselves, race track operators, etc.).

** Simulcasting is programming thoroughbred, harness, or quarter horse races which are shown on televisions or television projectors at a site away from the track for the purpose of pari-mutuel wagering. The person watching the television simulcasting is watching the race "live" and may bet on it as if he or she were at the track. Simulcasting may take place at an off-track betting branch, another race track which may or may not be having a meet of its own, or at a simulcast theater.

TABLE 4.2

	ON-TRACK ATTENDANCE					ON-TRACK AVERAGE ATTENDANCE				
	Total	Thoroughbred	Qtr. Horse	Harness	Mixed	Total	Thoroughbred	Qtr. Horse	Harness	Mixed
Arizona	708,914				708,914	2,791				2,791
Arkansas	1,125,025	1,125,025				17,308	17,308			
Birmingham, AL	443,017	443,017				2,837	3,956			
California	13,735,972	10,568,863	895,214	648,738	1,326,139	14,323	21,856	5,506	4,822	9,650
Colorado	9,990	9,990				999	999			
Connecticut										
Delaware	701,530	589,626		111,904		2,560	3,931		902	
Florida	2,924,505	2,346,207		578,298		5,250	5,822		3,755	
Idaho										
Illinois	4,948,537	2,901,219		2,047,318		4,464	5,933		3,292	
Iowa	353,323			64,399	288,924	2,860			1,464	3,074
Kansas	463,272				463,272	4,064				4,064
Kentucky	2,709,573	2,183,870	17,040	508,663		4,680	7,662	416	1,988	
Louisiana	1,967,105	1,680,784	134,301		152,020	2,872	3,502	1,450		1,345
Maryland	2,987,129	2,083,784		903,345		6,124	7,523		2,952	
Massachusetts	124,000	124,000				6,526	6,526			
Michigan	2,860,440	832,187		1,803,129	25,124	2,836	4,506		2,656	546
Minnesota	710,710	502,960			207,750	5,625	5,715			6,110
Montana										
Nebraska	857,051	837,177	19,874			3,426	3,754	736		
Nevada										
New Hampshire	1,276,683	1,276,683				4,800	4,987			
New Jersey	5,358,778	2,473,755		2,885,023		6,304	7,341		5,624	
New Mexico	1,204,447				1,204,447	2,801				2,801
New York	6,985,165	4,575,862		2,409,303		4,313	9,674		2,033	
North Dakota										
Ohio	3,859,461	1,859,500	17,450	1,722,500	259,921	3,064	3,048	3,490	3,619	1,232
Oklahoma	1,946,295	1,221,795			724,500	5,332	10,267			2,945
Oregon										0
Pennsylvania	2,597,117	1,785,143		811,974		3,183	3,967		2,219	
South Dakota	19,000				19,000	1,357				1,357
Texas	340,739				340,739	3,015				3,015
Vermont										
Washington	1,495,760	1,335,657			160,103	5,328	6,300			2,820
West Virginia	1,160,209	1,160,209				2,448	2,448			
Wyoming	128,996				128,996	1,743				1,743
Totals	63,802,743	42,014,133	1,083,879	14,894,882	6,009,849	4,610	6,775	3,356	2,984	2,512

Source: *Pari-Mutuel Racing, 1990*, Association of Racing Commissioners International, Inc., Lexington, KY

1992.) Unless the greyhound industry can develop an effective OTB system, the future for greyhound racing looks bleak.

The future is already bleak for the nation's jai-alai industry. From just 1991 to 1992, the handle tumbled almost 13 percent from $488 million to $426 million. Jai-alai is played in only three states (Connecticut, Rhode Island, and Florida). About the only good news for the industry is that most of the activity is located in Southern Florida which has not yet introduced casino gambling. On the other hand, the opening of the large casino complex at Ledyard, Connecticut is likely to devastate operations in Connecticut and Rhode Island.

HORSE RACING
THE SPORT OF KINGS

Horse racing has changed over the centuries from a sport associated with the aristocracy into one of the most popular pastimes in America. The first known form of horse racing was practiced by the Sumerians over 6,000 years ago and was similar to the chariot races occasionally seen in the movies. "Flat Racing," in which a rider is mounted directly on the horse instead of sitting in a rig drawn by an animal, was first popularized about 3,000 years ago. The first recorded horse race took place in Greece about 600 B.C. Horse racing became one of the major diversions of the British royalty between the 12th and 17th centuries, and thereafter, horse racing was known as the "Sport of Kings."

Horse racing was popular in colonial America and, true to its English heritage, was limited to the aristocracy or "gentry." In early colonial days, concern over the lack of quality horses in America prompted colonial governors to sponsor races as a means of identifying the fastest horses for selective breeding. The first race track in America was

TABLE 4.3

	INTER-TRACK ATTENDANCE					OFF-TRACK ATTENDANCE				
	Total	Thoroughbred	Qtr. Horse	Harness	Mixed	Total	Thoroughbred	Qtr. Horse	Harness	Mixed
Arizona										
Arkansas	70,445	70,445								
Birmingham, AL	98,926	98,926								
California						5,358,037	4,106,416	349,879	331,841	569,901
Colorado	445	445								
Connecticut						389,580	239,376		150,204	
Delaware										
Florida										
Idaho	6,226				6,226					
Illinois	1,942,544	1,146,488		796,056						
Iowa										
Kansas										
Kentucky	3,149,205	2,960,704		188,501						
Louisiana						1,004,770				1,004,770
Maryland	905,183	905,183								
Massachusetts										
Michigan										
Minnesota	93,873				93,873					
Montana										
Nebraska	437,379	437,379								
Nevada										
New Hampshire										
New Jersey										
New Mexico	299,167				299,167					
New York	784,021	753,042		30,979						
North Dakota						61,320	21,462		6,132	33,726
Ohio										
Oklahoma										
Oregon										
Pennsylvania	233,216	233,216				321,398	216,737		104,661	
South Dakota						2,640	2,640			
Texas										
Vermont										
Washington										
West Virginia	5,675	5,675								
Wyoming						55,967				55,967
Totals	8,026,305	6,611,504	0	1,015,535	399,266	7,193,712	4,586,631	349,679	592,838	1,664,364

Source: *Pari-Mutuel Racing, 1990*, Association of Racing Commissioners International, Inc., Lexington, KY

the Newmarket Course, built in 1665 in Hempstead, New York.

By the 1800s, horse racing was conducted at county fairs or at gypsy (traveling) tracks, most notably in Maryland, Virginia, and Kentucky. The first big race tracks opened around the turn of the century, with New York's Belmont Park leading the way in 1905. The first American stakes race, offering a purse for the winner, was the Traveler's Stakes at Saratoga Springs, New York. In 1934, California's Santa Anita track opened. The largest track in the United States, New York's Aqueduct, opened in 1959. Race tracks are usually operated by private investors but are regulated by State Racing Commissions.

Horseracing's popularity has been dropping over the past decade, a decline from which it may not recover. Average attendance at two of the country's most famous tracks, Aqueduct and Belmont Park in New York, has decreased 40 percent in the past 15 years, and attendance is down at many other tracks. Florida's Hialeah track, another stalwart of the industry, closed in 1990. Off-track betting and simulcasting helped start the decline, but the introduction of state lotteries and casino gambling nearly everywhere in the country has captured many gambling dollars that were once bet on the horses.

Types of Horse Racing Events

There are three major forms of horse racing: thoroughbred, harness, and quarter horse racing. Thoroughbred is, by far, the most popular form of horse racing, followed by harness and then quarter horse racing.

TABLE 4.4

	PARI-MUTUEL HANDLE: ALL FORMS OF BETTING ($)					HANDLE RETURNED TO BETTORS: TOTAL ($)				
	Total	Thoroughbred	Qtr. Horse	Harness	Mixed	Total	Thoroughbred	Qtr. Horse	Harness	Mixed
Arizona	86,748,926				86,748,926	87,717,870				87,747,870
Arkansas	145,267,243	145,267,243				110,481,662	110,481,662			
Birmingham, AL	67,679,207	65,297,866	2,381,341			40,161,619	40,161,619			
California	2,881,906,858	2,398,132,469	142,895,060	113,423,546	227,455,753	2,334,747,378	1,949,979,566	114,924,480	88,116,654	181,726,678
Colorado	522,259	522,259				396,040	396,040			
Connecticut	195,548,150				195,548,150	156,953,228				156,953,228
Delaware	94,271,637	83,936,118		10,335,519		75,360,820	67,402,470		7,958,350	
Florida	522,515,547	453,926,446		68,589,101		407,899,575	354,941,672		52,957,903	
Idaho	9,241,148	6,743,837	2,258,627		238,684	7,162,789	5,228,946	1,748,895		184,948
Illinois	1,252,368,115	720,925,204		531,442,911		982,664,662	567,626,014		415,038,648	
Iowa	30,365,277	2,893,167	39,800	3,200,983	25,231,335	24,855,700	2,368,217	32,579	1,801,634	20,653,300
Kansas	43,873,922				43,873,922	34,921,874				34,921,874
Kentucky	501,114,487	435,197,599	1,233,019	64,683,869		369,942,228	369,942,228			
Louisiana	627,915,237	545,889,823	25,849,138		56,176,276	498,991,148	465,533,160	13,820,169		19,637,819
Maryland	708,716,877	580,594,495		128,122,382		455,116,335	354,443,888		100,671,447	
Massachusetts	11,703,669	11,703,669				9,389,577	9,389,577			
Michigan	440,889,684	150,385,824		288,996,973	1,506,887	352,940,383	120,440,886		231,293,682	1,205,800
Minnesota	101,754,579	94,785,125	6,969,454			79,815,047	60,025,258	152,526		19,637,281
Montana	9,647,489				9,647,489	7,525,042				7,525,042
Nebraska	125,647,929	125,194,084	453,845			100,444,025	100,080,947	363,078		
Nevada	420,541				420,541	335,497				
New Hampshire	201,013,970			1,411,373		154,481,160	153,329,608		1,151,552	
New Jersey	1,177,841,492	635,808,297		541,033,195		942,071,402	434,261,993		507,809,409	
New Mexico	161,480,205				161,480,205	126,814,205				126,814,205
New York	3,326,000,805	2,591,818,557		734,182,248		2,693,012,336	2,104,678,130		588,334,206	
North Dakota	3,778,783	1,273,914		414,672	2,090,197	2,996,152	977,824		314,303	1,804,025
Ohio	461,768,546	260,541,984	133,748	195,069,858	6,022,956	364,259,533	205,840,505	105,693	153,560,783	4,752,552
Oklahoma	240,179,631	182,793,979	50,181,517		7,204,135	190,961,726	124,196,342			66,765,363
Oregon	39,132,528				39,132,528	30,756,706				30,756,706
Pennsylvania	448,621,343	335,050,922		113,570,421		363,265,468	290,542,671		72,722,797	
South Dakota	684,642	430,692	250,314		3,636	484,455				484,455
Texas	31,570,255				31,570,255	25,566,824				25,566,824
Vermont	1,046,265			1,046,265		793,618			793,618	
Washington	220,993,840	218,512,720			2,481,120	178,056,947	176,057,884			1,999,063
West Virginia	143,524,762	143,524,762				114,692,534	113,480,143			
Wyoming	11,290,180				11,290,180	8,869,184				8,869,184
Totals	$14,328,457,401	$10,290,165,046	$232,645,863	$2,894,523,515	$906,123,175	$11,314,636,587	$8,181,809,250	$131,147,420	$2,222,524,986	$777,944,668

Source: *Pari-Mutuel Racing, 1990,* Association of Racing Commissioners International, Inc., Lexington, KY

Thoroughbred Racing

Anatomically, the thoroughbred horse is distinguished from other breeds of horses by its greater height and longer legs, although in order to be registered as a thoroughbred, other criteria must be met. In 1894, the prestigious Jockey Club was formed in New York for the purpose of organizing and regulating thoroughbred racing. Traditionally, a thoroughbred horse must be registered with the New York Jockey Club, and a horse may be registered only if his sire (father) and dam (mother) are already on the rolls. In other words, the lineage of all thoroughbreds must be genetically traceable back to three oriental stallions, Godolphin, Byerly, and Darley, the prototypes of the breed.

Harness Racing

In harness racing, the rider sits in a carriage (sulky) and guides the horse around the track. The horses are trained to be either trotters or pacers. On a trotter, the left-front and right-rear legs of the horse move forward almost simultaneously, then the right-front and left-rear legs move. On a pacer, both left legs move forward in unison, then both right legs move.

Quarter Horse Racing

The quarter horse (the word quarter referring to the quarter-mile sprint it runs) was evolved in colonial Virginia where breeders crossed native English horses with those of Spanish ancestry. This cross-breeding resulted in a swift horse that could outrun other breeds in short-distance races. Unlike the thoroughbred, quarter horses can be used for farm work and transportation.

Racing Days and Number of Races

Race tracks are not open every day of the year, but rather operate for relatively short periods called "meets." A track might have two meets in a year, often one in the spring and one in the fall. State regulatory agencies usually approve the times for these meets and try to schedule them so that neighboring tracks do not have conflicting meets.

In 1990, there were a total of 13,841 racing days in the United States, down 3 percent from only the year before. New York had the greatest number of racing days (1,658), followed by Ohio (1,302), Illinois (1,111) and California (959), while Connecticut (0), North Dakota (8), Vermont (10), and Colorado (10) had the fewest (Table 4.1). Not surprisingly, some of these same states also had the greatest number of races in 1990, with 17,765 in New York, 11,719 in Illinois, 10,006 in California, 9,250 in Ohio, and 9,070 in Pennsylvania. Connecticut (0), North Dakota (85), Vermont (111), and Colorado (115) had the fewest. (See Table 4.1.)

Attendance

More than 63.8 million people attended a horse racing event at the track in 1990 (Table 4.2), while another 7.2 million watched the races at off-track betting parlors and another 8 million viewed a simulcast facility at another race track (Table 4.3). Daily average attendance totaled 4,610 (Table 4.2). Although New York had the most races and the most racing days that year, over 13.7 million people in California attended races in their state, compared to almost 7 million in New York. However, Arkansas had the highest daily average attendance (17,308). Among the states reporting attendance, Colorado had the lowest total attendance (9,990) and the lowest daily average attendance (999) (Table 4.2).

TABLE 4.5
HORSE RACING IN THE UNITED STATES

RACING REVENUE TO GOVERNMENT BY YEARS (1934-1990)

Year	Revenue	Year	Revenue	Year	Revenue	Year	Revenue
1990	623,839,806						
1989	584,888,183	1975	675,466,247	1961	264,853,077	1947	97,926,984
1988	596,202,319	1974	567,132,384	1960	258,039,385	1946	94,035,859
1987	608,351,461	1973	533,500,015	1959	243,388,655	1945	65,265,405
1986	587,357,677	1972	505,904,550	1958	222,049,651	1944	55,971,233
1985	625,159,697	1971	508,338,417	1957	216,747,621	1943	38,194,727
1984	650,262,852	1970	486,403,097	1956	207,456,272	1942	22,005,278
1983	641,387,176	1969	461,498,886	1955	186,989,588	1941	21,128,173
1982	652,888,463	1968	426,856,448	1954	178,015,828	1940	16,145,182
1981	680,199,584	1967	394,381,913	1953	167,426,465	1939	10,369,807
1980	712,727,523	1966	388,452,125	1952	142,489,696	1938	9,576,335
1979	680,919,798	1965	369,892,036	1951	117,250,564	1937	8,434,792
1978	673,063,831	1964	350,095,928	1950	98,366,167	1936	8,611,538
1977	700,239,986	1963	316,570,791	1949	95,327,053	1935	8,386,255
1976	714,629,120	1962	287,930,030	1948	95,803,364	1934	6,024,193

(These statistics do not include revenue produced by off-track betting in New York from 1971 -1975.)

Source: *Pari-Mutuel Racing, 1990*, Association of Racing Commissioners International, Inc., Lexington, KY

Horse Racing Handle

Pari-mutuel bettors wagered $14.3 billion on horse races in 1990-78 percent of all the money wagered on all pari-mutuel events for the year. About $8.9 billion was bet at the track, $260 million was wagered on simulcast racing events at a racetrack holding races, $1.4 billion was bet on inter-track races where races are transmitted to other tracks that are not holding live races but show the races on large screens, and $3.9 billion was wagered at off-track betting establishments.

Only about 61 percent of all money legally bet on horseraces is bet at the track in which the horserace is taking place. The total handle for thoroughbred racing far exceeded the handle for either harness racing or quarter horse racing. New York races took in almost 23 percent of the total 1990 handle ($3.3 billion) and California took in 20 percent ($2.9 billion) (Table 4.4).

Government Revenues

In 1990, state governments netted $623 million from pari-mutuel betting on horse races. Horseracing revenue to government peaked at $715 million in 1976 and $713 million in 1980 and have been generally sliding downward ever since. The revenue increase from 1989 to 1990 was only the second time in a decade revenues increased over the previous year. Table 4.5 shows government horse racing revenue from 1934 through 1990. Table 4.6 shows how much each state got from horseracing. California ($199 million) and New York ($195 million) got almost two-thirds of all the revenues gained by the states.

State governments collected $31 million in uncashed pari-mutuel tickets, that is, winnings that were never claimed! Forty-three percent of all uncashed tickets were from New York State.

Return to Bettors and to the Winning Horse Owners

An average of 79 percent ($11.3 billion) of the $14.3 billion wagered on pari-mutuel horse races in 1990 was returned to the bettors. Owners of winning horses claimed nearly $951 million in prize money in 1990.

DOG RACING — THE SPORT OF QUEENS

Dog racing developed from a hunting sport called "coursing" in which a hare was released and then a pair of greyhounds was set in pursuit. The race was judged on the dogs' performance as they ran down the hare. Coursing was very popular during the reign of Queen Elizabeth I of England, in the last half of the 16th century. For this reason, it became known as the "Sport of Queens." The modern version of dog racing developed from a coursing event in South Dakota in 1904. The sponsor of the contest, Owen Patrick Smith, loved the sport, but detested the killing of the hare. Smith spent 15 years perfecting a mechanical lure, thus eliminating one of the more inhumane aspects of the sport.

TABLE 4.6
TOTAL REVENUE TO GOVERNMENT($)

Total	Total	Thoroughbred	Qtr. Horse	Harness	Mixed
Arizona	921,480				921,480
Arkansas	5,027,087	5,027,087			
Birmingham, AL	1,472,505	1,406,002	66,503		
California	198,849,806	173,816,174	4,221,905	4,236,946	16,574,581
Colorado	47,363	47,363			
Connecticut	910,024				910,024
Delaware	407,374	344,796		62,578	
Florida	12,549,866	11,419,003		1,130,863	
Idaho	352,327	186,974	64,462		100,891
Illinois	49,047,872	28,540,537		20,507,335	
Iowa	288,396			50,083	238,313
Kansas	1,567,890				1,567,890
Kentucky	26,266,579	25,193,173	75,967	996,439	
Louisiana	26,945,613	21,939,247	566,060		4,440,306
Maryland	5,771,735	4,497,343		1,274,392	
Massachusetts	987,074	987,074			
Michigan	22,089,435	7,958,197		14,042,279	88,959
Minnesota	2,007,581	957,112	6,098		1,046,371
Montana	147,675				147,675
Nebraska	784,635	290,899			493,736
Nevada	14,127				14,127
New Hampshire	4,701,512	4,654,351		47,161	
New Jersey	9,434,794	5,061,182		4,373,612	
New Mexico	763,234				763,234
New York	194,735,524	164,139,153		30,596,371	
North Dakota	228,322	80,540		10,187	137,595
Ohio	21,392,229	11,305,406	9,788	9,796,542	280,493
Oklahoma	10,622,006	6,985,027			3,636,979
Oregon	952,779				952,779
Pennsylvania	8,919,175	7,677,215		1,241,960	
South Dakota	25,964	1,004			24,960
Texas	1,990,709				1,990,709
Vermont	41,046			41,046	
Washington	11,269,734	11,158,784			110,950
West Virginia	2,263,961	2,263,961			
Wyoming	243,573				243,573
Totals	623,839,604	$495,937,604	5,010,783	$88,407,794	34,483,625

Source: *Pari-Mutuel Racing, 1990*, Association of Racing Commissioners International, Inc., Lexington, KY.

Dog racing today normally refers to greyhound racing. The sport has grown in popularity, and both the number of tracks and attendance more than doubled in the past 20 years, and handle increased by over 500 percent. Nonetheless, while track attendance and the number of meets and races continues to rise, some owners recognize that the rise in lotteries and casino gambling represent a serious danger for the future of their industry.

Total Performances, Number of Races, and Attendance

As indicated earlier, greyhound racing is facing serious difficulties which are reflected in the drop in virtually all financial categories from 1991 to 1992. During 1992, 17,407 performances or races took place, up 3 percent from the year before. Over one-fourth (26 percent) of all races were held in Florida. Total attendance fell almost 6 per-

TABLE 4.7

1992 RECAPITULATION

STATE	NITES	MATS.	TOTAL PERF.	ATTENDANCE	REVENUE TO GOVERNMENTS	PURSE DISTRIBUTION	P/M HANDLE
Alabama	951	568	1,519	2,166,509	$ 19,535,707	$ 8,758,476	$ 308,046,109
Arizona	725	372	1,097	1,178,630	7,064,851	4,104,521	136,984,533
Arkansas	258	131	389	1,479,129	15,427,783	7,021,446	198,837,141
Colorado	573	247	820	1,397,719	9,196,973	6,907,737	166,711,297
Connecticut	180	259	439	520,355	4,145,148	2,694,965	78,214,639
Florida	3,094	1,437	4,531	8,062,969	72,164,234	35,030,791	883,126,895
Idaho	301	104	405	309,982	881,092	611,427	20,380,907
Iowa	553	382	935	969,884	6,058,023	4,165,872	96,638,531
Kansas	477	315	792	1,811,797	8,757,122	9,281,514	203,542,502
Massachusetts	601	498	1,099	2,536,616	20,149,966	13,662,523	312,970,890
New Hampshire	425	601	1,026	848,538	4,310,232	3,206,071	73,041,062
Oregon	92	98	190	550,054	3,530,291	2,411,966	56,089,124
Rhode Island	194	278	472	1,065,502	6,660,366	5,229,665	106,646,983
South Dakota	80	0	80	28,503	518,856	204,403	9,351,447
Texas	627	313	940	1,619,591	5,004,361	6,842,409	143,223,310
Vermont	78	27	105	92,815	203,310	290,119	6,652,485
West Virginia	585	177	762	986,646	7,844,869	4,691,514	122,577,025
Wisconsin	966	840	1,806	3,065,338	15,842,152	14,338,570	303,658,177
Nat'l. Totals	10,760	6,647	17,407	28,690,577	$207,295,336	$129,453,989	$3,226,693,057

COMPARATIVE DATA

	NITES	MATS.	TOTAL PERF.	ATTENDANCE	REVENUE TO GOVERNMENTS	PURSE DISTRIBUTION	P/M HANDLE
1991	10,755	6,072	16,827	30,454,685	$233,662,121	N/A	$3,475,865,504
1992	10,760	6,647	17,407	28,690,577	207,295,336	129,453,989	3,226,693,057
Difference	+5	+575	+580	−1,764,108	$−26,366,785		$ −249,172,447
Percentage	0.0%	+9.5%	+3.4%	−5.8%	−11.3%		−7.2%

	1991	1992
Average attendance per performance	1,809	1,648
Average revenue to governments per performance	$ 13,886	$ 11,908
Average pari-mutuel handle per performance	$ 206,306	$ 185,368
Average per capita per attendee	$ 114	$ 112

Source: 1992—*Summary of State Pari-Mutuel Tax Structures*, American Greyhound Track Operators Association, North Miami, FL.

cent from 30.5 million in 1991 to 28.7 million in 1992. Average on track attendance dropped 9 percent from 1,809 in 1991 to 1,648 in 1992 (Table 4.7).

The Handle, Government Revenues, and Purses to the Winning Dog Owners

Bettors placed $3.2 billion on dog races in 1992, down 7 percent from almost $3.5 billion in

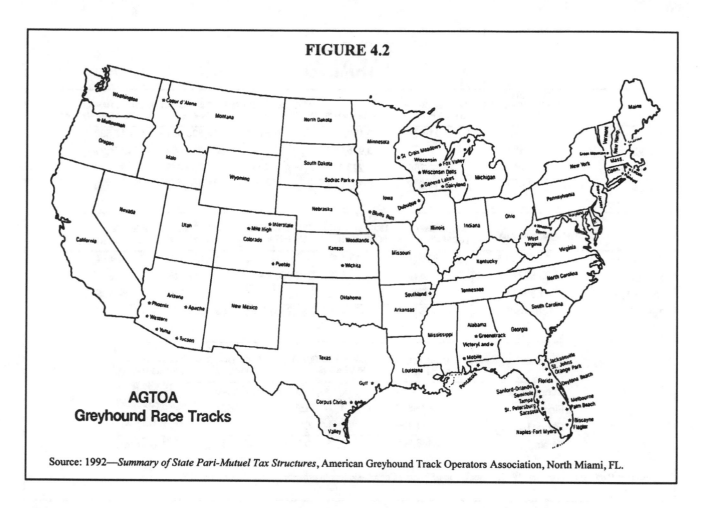

FIGURE 4.2

AGTOA
Greyhound Race Tracks

Source: 1992—*Summary of State Pari-Mutuel Tax Structures*, American Greyhound Track Operators Association, North Miami, FL.

1991. With the handle dropping, government revenues fell 11 percent from $233.7 million in 1991 to $207.3 million in 1992. Almost $129.5 million went to the winning owners. Overall, about 82 percent of the handle is returned to the bettors, 6 percent to the government, 4 percent to purses for the winning owners, and 8 percent to the track owners for operating expenses and profit.

Greyhound Racing by State

Figure 4.2 shows the locations of the nation's 59 greyhound racing tracks. Florida has, by far, the most attendance (28 percent) and handle (27 percent). Other major states are Wisconsin, Massachusetts, and Alabama (Table 4.7).

JAI-ALAI

Jai-alai, which means "merry festival," is a fast-paced game in which the players, using large curved baskets (called a "cesta") strapped to their arms, whip a small hard ball ("pelota") made of goat skin against the three walls and floor of a huge playing court ("fronton") in much the same manner as handball or racquetball. Jai-alai was invented in the 17th century by the Basques, who live in northern Spain and southern France. It has been a popular game in Latin America during recent years and is gaining in popularity in the United States. Pari-mutuel betting on jai-alai is available in three states, Connecticut, Florida, and Rhode Island. Jai-alai has never gained a following outside of southern New England and Florida.

In addition, all betting takes place at the jai-alai fronton; there is no off-track betting (or more properly off-fronton betting) to help increase declining revenues as has been the case with horse racing. The introduction of casino gambling at Ledyard, Connecticut is sure to add to jai-alai's woes. While Florida, especially Dade and Broward counties in the southern part of the state (the Miami and Fort Lauderdale area), has chosen not to

TABLE 4.8
JAI-ALAI

	NUMBER OF PERFORMANCES HELD	NUMBER OF GAMES PLAYED	ATTENDANCE	AVERAGE ATTENDANCE PER PERFORMANCE	PARI-MUTUEL HANDLE ($)	AVERAGE HANDLE PER PERFORMANCE ($)
Connecticut	787	11,537	1,190,923	1,513	194,835,951	247,568
Florida	2,584		3,915,056	1,515	329,530,604	127,527
Rhode Island	248	3,264	223,117	900	21,089,643	85,039
Totals	3,619	14,801	5,329,096	1,473	$545,456,198	$150,720

	TOTAL REVENUE ($)	% INCREASE/ DECREASE	OCCUPATIONAL LICENSE REVENUE ($)	FRANCHISE FEE REVENUE ($)	PARI-MUTUEL TAX REVENUE ($)	BREAKAGE REVENUE ($)
Connecticut	13,772,213	-7.07%	13,430		13,151,428	123,434
Florida	25,532,044	1.54%	50,873	2,250,830	19,251,246	468,543
Rhode Island	1,304,064	24.47%	4,422		1,265,378	14,505
Totals	$38,608,321	-0.75%	$68,725	$2,250,830	$33,668,052	$606,482

	ADMISSION TAX REVENUE ($)	UNCASHED TICKET REVENUE ($)	MISCELLANEOUS REVENUE ($)	PURSE DISTRIBUTION ($)
Connecticut		481,481	2,440	16,522,637
Florida	475,813	1,007,115	27,624	5,208,765
Rhode Island	11,156	8,603		1,374,996
Totals	$486,969	$1,497,199	$30,064	$23,106,398

Source: *Pari-Mutuel Racing, 1990*, Association of Racing Commissioners International, Inc., Lexington, KY.

introduce casino gambling, which offers jai-alai a respite from the challenge of casino gambling, the future of the sport in the United States is very uncertain.

Number of Performances, Number of Games, and Attendance

During 1990, there were 3,619 performances or events. Seventy-one percent of these performances took place in Florida. Florida accounted for 74 percent of total attendance, 3.9 million attendees out of 5.3 million, although daily attendance at the games in Connecticut (1,513) was virtually the same as in Florida (1,515) (Table 4.8).

TABLE 4.9
JAI-ALAI REVENUE TO GOVERNMENT (1978 - 1990)

1990	$38,608,321
1989	38,898,706
1988	43,572,178
1987	51,377,135
1986	50,144,777
1985	50,079,524
1984	48,269,509
1983	45,398,087
1982	45,000,544
1981	44,364,100
1980	35,308,705
1979	36,036,607
1978	34,707,615

NOTE: Data unavailable for Nevada

Source: *Pari-Mutuel Racing, 1990*, Association of Racing Commissioners International, Inc., Lexington, KY

TABLE 4.10
HORSE RACING IN CANADA

	RACING DAYS			NUMBER OF RACES		
	TOTAL	THOROUGHBRED	HARNESS	TOTAL	THOROUGHBRED	HARNESS
Alberta	441	239	202	5,490	2,644	2,846
British Columbia	340	165	175	3,427	1,586	1,841
Manitoba	240	119	121	2,507	1,232	1,275
New Brunswick	208	0	208	2,152	0	2,152
Newfoundland	42	0	42	395	0	395
Nova Scotia	241	0	241	2,595	0	2,595
Ontario	1,898	313	1,585	20,416	3,154	17,262
Prince Edward Island	149	0	149	1,742	0	1,742
Quebec	668	0	668	7,719	426	7,293
Saskatchewan	149	76	73	1,509	823	686
Totals	4,376	912	3,464	47,952	9,865	38,087

	ATTENDANCE			DAILY AVERAGE ATTENDANCE		
	TOTAL	THOROUGHBRED	HARNESS	TOTAL	THOROUGHBRED	HARNESS
Alberta	1,216,586	639,137	577,449	5,533	2,674	2,859
British Columbia	1,220,027	820,099	399,928	7,256	4,970	2,285
Manitoba	452,313	299,430	152,883	3,780	2,516	1,263
New Brunswick	126,871	0	126,871	610	0	610
Newfoundland	13,596	0	13,596	324	0	324
Nova Scotia	105,283	0	105,283	437	0	437
Ontario	6,075,808	2,369,454	3,706,354	9,909	7,570	2,338
Prince Edward Island	79,850	0	79,850	536	0	536
Quebec	1,929,686	104,420	1,825,266	2,732	0	2,732
Saskatchewan	128,416	69,195	59,221	1,722	910	811
Totals	11,348,436	4,301,735	7,046,701	5,751	4,717	2,034

Source: *Pari-Mutuel Racing, 1990*, Association of Racing Commissioners International, Inc., Lexington, KY.

Handle and Government Revenue

Pari-mutuel handle for jai-alai games in 1990 was $545.5 million, down from $552.7 million in 1989 and $639.2 million in 1988 (Table 4.8). Government revenue totaled $38.6 million, down only slightly from $38.9 million in 1989, but sharply from the $51.4 million in 1987 (Table 4.9).

HORSE RACING IN CANADA

Harness racing is the most popular form of the sport in Canada. Almost 11.4 million people visited Canadian horse racing tracks to attend 47,952 races in 1990 (Table 4.10).

The pari-mutuel handle totaled nearly $2 billion, producing $141.7 million for the government

TABLE 4.11

	PARI-MUTUEL HANDLE ($): ALL FORMS OF BETTING			TOTAL REVENUE TO JURISDICTIONS/GOVERNMENT ($)		
	TOTAL	THOROUGHBRED	HARNESS	TOTAL	THOROUGHBRED	HARNESS
Alberta	210,547,623	102,324,209	108,223,414	10,527,381	5,116,210	5,411,171
British Columbia	211,982,216	151,458,575	60,523,641	14,838,755	10,602,100	4,236,655
Manitoba	58,526,484	39,276,051	19,250,433	5,485,892	3,599,650	1,886,242
New Brunswick	11,144,680	0	11,144,680	1,225,915	0	1,225,915
Newfoundland	779,772	0	779,772	85,775	0	85,775
Nova Scotia	12,278,942	0	12,278,942	1,350,684	0	1,350,684
Ontario	1,151,749,593	536,349,560	615,400,033	85,285,620	39,234,770	46,050,850
Prince Edward Island	7,016,785	0	7,016,785	944,820	0	944,820
Quebec	315,340,163	17,364,224	297,976,504	21,023,973	1,243,378	19,780,595
Saskatchewan	9,655,163	5,864,264	3,790,899	965,516	586,426	379,090
Totals	$1,989,021,986	$852,636,883	$1,136,385,103	$141,734,331	$60,382,534	$81,351,797

	TOTAL PURSE MONEY DISTRIBUTED ($)			HANDLE RETURNED TO BETTORS
	TOTAL	THOROUGHBRED	HARNESS	ALL BREEDS
Alberta	16,795,302	8,441,611	8,353,691	158,480,469
British Columbia	14,657,421	9,491,739	5,165,682	154,946,884
Manitoba	6,045,287	4,230,649	1,814,638	39,889,229
New Brunswick	2,589,171	0	2,589,171	9,025,266
Newfoundland	90,540	0	90,540	490,412
Nova Scotia	1,728,054	0	1,728,054	7,761,219
Ontario	114,319,566	45,515,155	68,804,411	822,023,344
Prince Edward Island	1,188,492	0	1,188,492	4,342,689
Quebec	30,536,622	0	30,536,622	225,550,072
Saskatchewan	2,022,145	1,173,560	848,585	6,432,096
Totals	$189,972,600	$68,852,714	$121,119,886	$1,428,941,662

Source: *Pari-Mutuel Racing, 1990*, Association of Racing Commissioners International, Inc.

and local jurisdictions, $1.43 billion for winning bettors, and $190 million in purses for winning owners (Table 4.11).

HORSE RACING IN PUERTO RICO, MEXICO, AND JAMAICA

In Puerto Rico, 482,409 people attended 1,505 races on the Commonwealth of Puerto Rico's 188 racing days for an average daily attendance of 2,566 horseracing fans. The bettors placed $143.7 million in bets. The Commonwealth received $23.2 million dollars, and $16.5 million was paid to the winning horseowners.

In Mexico, 1.6 million people attended 3,123 races on Mexico's 249 racing days for an average attendance of 6,477 fans. The bettors placed $71.8 million in bets. The Mexican government received $26.1 million, and $5.2 million was paid to the winning owners.

In Jamaica, 125,000 people attended 643 races on Jamaica's 64 racing days for an average attendance of 1,953 fans. The bettors placed $27.5 million in bets. The Jamaican government received $3.9 million, and $1.4 million was paid to the winning owners.

CHAPTER V

CASINO GAMBLING

EXPLODING INTO AMERICAN LIFE

Technically, a casino is any room or rooms in which gaming is conducted. However, when most Americans think of casinos they picture the gaudy hotel/casino/entertainment complexes seen on TV and movie screens. For many years, casinos were associated exclusively with Nevada and especially Las Vegas. In 1977, the state of New Jersey legalized casino gambling for Atlantic City.

Over the past decade local and state governments have increasingly turned to gambling in an effort to increase revenues. Lotteries have been the most public form of gambling, but an increasing number of state and local governments have turned to casino gambling in order to raise money without raising taxes.

Although the recent development of casinos has been most popular in the Midwest, the issue has been raised throughout the country. Not only are casinos now located in cities such as Deadwood, South Dakota and Cripple Creek, Colorado, but casinos now float up and down the Mississippi and Missouri Rivers and out into the Gulf of Mexico and the Pacific and Atlantic Oceans.

In addition, many Native American tribes have begun to introduce casino gambling onto their reservations in an effort to raise money. While these new casinos generate only a small percentage of the total amount earned by casinos, this sector of the market is growing rapidly, and the management of several Las Vegas gambling casinos have shown an interest in helping to develop the new casinos.

CASINOS IN NEVADA
A CENTURY OF GAMBLING

Nevadans adopted gambling as a way of life long before the state was admitted to the Union. Casinos were located in gold mining camps and were considered a major source of entertainment, but there were few professional gamblers. By 1869, the Nevada legislature had legalized gambling in the state, and, except for a few periods of reform, casinos and Nevada have been linked ever since. Within the past 100 years, a pastime that mainly served to separate miners and cowboys from their money has become a respected state industry. Today, casino gambling is the main pillar of Nevada's economy, attracting residents and tourists alike, and, with them, so many dollars that neither individuals nor corporations pay any state income taxes.

CASINOS IN NEW JERSEY

At the turn of the 20th century, Atlantic City, New Jersey, was a famous seaside resort that attracted thousands of tourists to its Boardwalk on the ocean front. But by the 1950s its glory had faded. Cars and planes allowed East Coast residents to travel to more exotic shores and the city did not have an alternate economy to make up for the lost tourist dollars. In an attempt to rebuild the city's financial base, lower taxes, provide employment for its residents, and subsidize its considerable elderly population, the State of New Jersey legalized gambling in Atlantic City on June 2, 1977. All funds raised from the licensing and taxation of gambling operations were to be used for state and local social programs. As the "East Coast Vegas," Atlantic City once again became a mecca —this time for gamblers and East Coast day-trippers.

AND NOW CASINOS
ARE ALMOST EVERYWHERE

During the 1980s, as federal funding for state and local projects have been cut, as financial demands have increased upon state and local governments, as many manufacturing companies have moved elsewhere in search of cheaper labor and more concessions, and as areas dependent upon agriculture have suffered severe economic reverses, many states and localities began to consider various forms of gambling to raise money, especially since raising taxes was politically very unpopular. Lotteries had already gotten most state governments into the gambling business, so other methods of gambling more easily appeared as a sensible alternative.

By the early 1990s, card rooms where players could gamble on card games were booming in California, Oregon, Washington, and Montana. Casinos were attracting players in South Dakota and Colorado, while riverboat gamblers could place wagers on the river waterways of Illinois, Iowa, and Mississippi (and, by 1994, in Louisiana). By November 19, 1993, 78 tribes in 18 states had approval to operate gambling establishments on their reservations (this does not include bingo). Meanwhile, many cruise lines have added or expanded casino operations in order to earn more money from existing cruises, while other cruise ships are floating casinos that sail out into the Atlantic Ocean or Gulf of Mexico so that their passengers can gamble outside United States waters.

REGULATIONS

For many years, casino gambling in Las Vegas has been associated with organized crime. In 1959, the State of Nevada created the State Gaming Control Board which is responsible for establishing gambling policy and suspending or revok-

ing licenses for any cause it considers reasonable. In 1976, New Jersey formed the New Jersey Casino Control Commission (NJCCC) to be responsible for monitoring gambling activities, which are permitted only in casino rooms located within approved hotels in Atlantic City. The Control Commission strictly controls the extension of credit to gamblers and the collection of gambling funds.

States new to gambling have been setting up gambling control boards or commissions to regulate gambling. Many of these new states have put limits on how much can be bet in order to make the new gambling operations less attractive to organized crime. However, these limitations may change as competition may force some states to increase gambling limits. For example, Illinois does not limit the amount a person may bet or lose on riverboats based in that state. On the other side of the river in Iowa, the limit is $5.00 per bet and $200.00 losses per day. The Iowa legislature may have to reconsider its limits if many gamblers choose to spend their money on Illinois-based riverboats.

Because of the potential risk of stealing by the gambling patrons or the casino itself, all games are closely monitored. The gambling area is carefully watched and video-taped to guarantee that none of the casino employees steal from either the customers or their employers. State auditors conduct regular, unannounced audits and check the casinos' internal control systems. In every instance where money is counted and transferred from one station to another, two or more people are involved so they can check on each other, thus lessening the likelihood of "skimming" — the practice of reporting less money than is actually collected from the gamblers.

CASINO GAMES

Slot Machines

Slot machines are vending-like machines into which the player drops a coin or dollar bill, pulls a lever, or pushes a button and hopes to "hit the jackpot" by releasing a large amount of money from

TABLE 5.1

Trends in Nevada and New Jersey Casino Win
1982 – 1992 (Calendar Years)

Game	1982 Reported Win ($)	1991 Reported Win ($)	% Change Over 1990	1992 Reported Win ($)	% Change Over 1991	Analysis % Change Over 1982	1982 Market Share	1992 Market Share	Gains (Losses) in Market Share Points 1982-1992
Blackjack	$984,781,664	1,380,925,000	-5.85%	$1,351,475,085	-2.13%	37.24%	23.50%	15.10%	(8.40)
Craps	620,879,078	733,500,000	-9.40%	703,604,462	-4.08%	13.32%	14.82%	7.86%	(6.96)
Roulette	133,096,939	260,478,000	-0.40%	268,021,555	2.90%	101.37%	3.18%	2.99%	(0.18)
Baccarat	225,611,107	478,623,000	-11.65%	375,409,420	-21.56%	66.40%	5.38%	4.19%	(1.19)
Mini-Baccarat		20,586,000	28.50%	62,001,387	201.18%	N/A		0.69%	0.69
Big Six	30,697,182	33,127,000	-9.44%	29,087,229	-12.19%	-5.24%	0.73%	0.32%	(0.41)
Keno	138,061,019	141,491,000	-0.60%	139,207,000	-1.61%	0.83%	3.29%	1.56%	(1.74)
Bingo	3,489,492	(4,759,000)	8.66%	965,000	120.28%	-72.35%	0.08%	0.01%	(0.07)
Pai Gow		22,536,000	4.23%	24,262,000	7.66%	N/A		0.27%	0.27
Sic Bo		951,000	-9.17%	926,000	-2.63%	N/A		0.01%	0.01
Pai Gow Poker		36,758,000	19.99%	41,462,000	12.80%	N/A		0.46%	0.46
Red Dog		3,719,000	-18.92%	4,047,000	8.82%	N/A		0.05%	0.05
Other	6,300,936	16,362,000	88.33%	44,968,261	174.83%	613.68%	0.15%	0.50%	0.35
Total Games	$2,142,917,417	$3,124,297,000	-6.34%	$3,045,436,399	-2.52%	42.12%	51.14%	34.02%	(17.12)
Card Tables									
Poker & Panguingui	55,761,646	76,671,000	7.48%	74,701,000	-2.57%	33.96%	1.33%	0.83%	(0.50)
Other	3,209								
Total Card Games	$55,764,855	$76,671,000	7.48%	$74,701,000	-2.57%	33.96%	1.33%	0.83%	(0.50)
Total Games	$2,198,682,272	$3,200,968,000	3.14%	$3,120,137,399	-2.53%	41.91%	52.47%	34.86%	(17.61)
Slot Machines	$1,991,456,185	$5,242,299,000	20.51%	$5,830,586,443	11.22%	192.78%	47.53%	65.14%	17.61
Total Casino	$4,190,138,457	$8,443,267,000	13.28%	$8,950,723,842	6.01%	113.61%	100.00%	100.00%	

Source: Eugene Martin Christiansen in *International Gaming & Wagering Business*, NY

the machine. Bettors can play for as little as 5 cents or try their luck on the $1 machines. The "pay-out" or jackpot, which is set by the casino and displayed on the machine, ranges from 78 percent to 97 percent, with an average of 85 percent being returned as payoff to players while management and the state take the rest.

Table Games

Table games include twenty-one, craps, roulette, baccarat, keno, and bingo. Not all types of games are available at all gambling establishments. The larger casinos and hotel/casino complexes generally offer the widest variety of table games.

FINANCIAL INFORMATION

The Nevada State Gaming Control Board and the NJCCC each issue an annual report of financial operations for casinos operating within their states. The Nevada report, *Nevada Gaming Abstract*, gives information on the "major" casinos, those that grossed $1 million or more during the year of the report. Atlantic City (the only city in New Jersey with legalized casino gambling) has far fewer casinos than Nevada. The NJCCC's *Annual Report* includes information on all casinos operating in Atlantic City during the year of the report. The NJCCC uses the calendar year as its fiscal year, while the Nevada Board's fiscal year runs from July 1 through June 30.

Most of the data in this chapter are taken from the 1992 *Nevada Gaming Abstract* and the NJCCC's 1992 *Annual Report*, the latest reports available. The South Dakota Commission on Gaming release showing gross revenue and "Colorado Gaming, Statistical Profile, 1991-1993" and "What are the Facts, 1992-1993," prepared by the Colorado Division of Gaming provided information on gambling in those states. Information on the other casino earnings is based upon reports of *Gaming and Wagering Business*.

CASINO REVENUES

In 1992, Americans bet $252.9 billion on casino games and slot machines. Almost all (95 percent) of it was bet on table games in Nevada and New Jersey ($143.1 billion) and slot machines in Nevada and New Jersey ($94.6 billion). Total casino win (the money won by the casino, not the gambler) has increased steadily over the past few years. Table 5.1 shows trends in U.S. casino win, by game, for the decade 1982 through 1992. During that period casino win more than doubled from $4.19 billion in 1982 to $8.95 billion in 1992.

TABLE 5.2

COMBINED INCOME STATEMENT - SUMMARY

Fiscal Year 1992
Statewide Casinos
With Gaming Revenue of $1,000,000 and over

AMOUNTS REPRESENT 192 LOCATION(S).

	DOLLARS	PCT
REVENUE		
GAMING	5,584,559,864	61.0
ROOMS	1,267,776,843	13.8
FOOD	1,101,621,195	12.0
BEVERAGE	524,422,399	5.7
OTHER	675,259,642	7.4
TOTAL REVENUE	9,153,639,943	100.0
COST OF SALES	818,188,047	8.9
GROSS MARGIN	8,335,451,896	91.1
DEPARTMENTAL EXPENSES	4,509,434,880	49.3
DEPARTMENTAL INCOME(- LOSS)	3,826,017,016	41.8
GENERAL AND ADMINISTRATIVE EXPENSES		
ADVERTISING AND PROMOTION	208,518,371	2.3
BAD DEBT EXPENSE	4,756,954	0.1
COMPLIMENTARY EXPENSE (not reported in operation departments)	106,824,376	1.2
DEPRECIATION - BUILDINGS	218,164,102	2.4
DEPRECIATION AND AMORTIZATION - OTHER	347,101,291	3.8
ENERGY EXPENSE (electricity,gas,etc.)	142,802,557	1.6
EQUIPMENT RENTAL OR LEASE	10,883,649	0.1
INTEREST EXPENSE	420,537,702	4.6
MUSIC AND ENTERTAINMENT	108,212,475	1.2
PAYROLL TAXES	56,729,761	0.6
PAYROLL - EMPLOYEE BENEFITS	126,560,679	1.4
PAYROLL - OFFICERS	45,992,826	0.5
PAYROLL - OTHER EMPLOYEES	504,619,970	5.5
RENT OF PREMISES	88,557,489	1.0
TAXES - REAL ESTATE	72,345,879	0.8
TAXES AND LICENSES - OTHER	13,918,895	0.2
UTILITIES (OTHER THAN ENERGY EXPENSE)	30,868,203	0.3
OTHER GENERAL & ADMINISTRATIVE EXPENSES	470,015,620	5.1
TOTAL GENERAL AND ADMINISTRATIVE EXPENSES	2,977,410,799	32.5
NET INCOME(- LOSS) BEFORE FEDERAL INCOME TAXES AND EXTRAORDINARY ITEMS	848,606,217	9.3

Source: *Nevada Gaming Abstract 1992*, State Gaming Control Board, (Carson City, NV 1993)

Since the house, on the average, keeps far more of the money bet on slot machines (6.17 percent in 1992) than it keeps on table games (2.18 percent), slot machines have become more profitable for the casino owners. Between 1982 and 1992, the win from slot machines rose 193 percent from $2 billion to $5.8 billion, while the win from games rose only 42 percent from $2.2 billion to $3.1 billion.

In fact, the return from the games dropped 2.5 percent from 1991 to 1992. Since 1983, casinos have earned more money from slot machines than they have earned from games. (See Table 5.1.) In 1982, games accounted for 52.5 percent of casino earnings, while slot machines brought in 47.5 percent. A decade later the situation was reversed with games accounting for just 35 percent and the slot machines bringing in 65 percent.

Nevada

The 192 major casinos operating in Nevada in 1992 (up from 169 locations in 1989 and 182 locations in 1990), produced $9.1 billion in gross revenues (up from $7.3 billion in 1989 and $8 billion in 1990). Net income (before federal income taxes and extraordinary items) for the year was $848,606,217, up from $545.9 million in 1990. The casinos' "Combined Income Statement — Summary" (Table 5.2) shows that gaming accounted for 61 percent ($5.6 billion) of total revenue. About 62 percent of gaming ("casino") revenue ($3.5 billion) came from slot machines ("coin-operated devices") and 34 percent ($1.9 billion) from pit revenue (Table 5.3). Table 5.4 shows gaming revenue per square foot of floor space.

In fiscal year 1992, almost 26 million rooms were filled in Nevada for an 86 percent occupancy rate. Except during the annual COMDEX computer convention held in the Fall, room rates in Nevada are generally inexpensive running about $49 per day, a far lower rate than that charged by most much less luxurious hotels in other cities. These low rates are meant to attract potential gamblers who, the hotel hopes, will spend a lot of money at the slot machines and gaming tables and, in fact, the average room produced $73.75 in revenues at the tables and $133.24 on the slot machines. Between the room charge, gambling revenues, and food and beverage sales, the hotels brought in an average of $334.72 per room per day in 1992. (See Table 5.5.)

Thirty-four of these 192 hotel/casinos are publicly-owned and have gross gaming revenues of $12 million or more. These larger facilities (often called the "Super Casinos") are owned by fifteen publicly-held corporations and include the more well-known casinos such as the Tropicana, Bally's, Caesar's Palace, Circus Circus, the Golden Nugget, the Mirage, and Harrah's. While these 34 hotel/resorts make up 18 percent of the total number of hotels, they account for 52 percent of the total gambling revenue.

TABLE 5.3
COMBINED INCOME STATEMENT - DETAIL

Fiscal Year 1992
Statewide Casinos
With Gaming Revenue of $1,000,000 and over

AMOUNTS REPRESENT 192 LOCATION(S).

CASINO DEPARTMENT

REVENUE	DOLLARS	PCT
PIT REVENUE (INCLUDES KENO AND BINGO) . . .	1,916,629,833	34.3
COIN OPERATED DEVICES	3,462,657,969	62.0
POKER AND PAN	78,013,226	1.4
RACE BOOK	81,932,722	1.5
SPORTS POOL	45,326,114	0.8
TOTAL REVENUE	5,584,559,864	100.0
DEPARTMENTAL EXPENSES		
BAD DEBT EXPENSE	105,276,379	1.9
COMMISSIONS	35,353,092	0.6
COMPLIMENTARY EXPENSE	642,520,126	11.5
GAMING TAXES AND LICENSES	432,694,855	7.7
JUNKET EXPENSES (no complimentaries)	16,812,944	0.3
PAYROLL TAXES	99,597,187	1.8
PAYROLL - EMPLOYEE BENEFITS	184,552,619	3.3
PAYROLL - OFFICERS	10,100,609	0.2
PAYROLL - OTHER EMPLOYEES	824,290,485	14.8
RACE WIRE FEES	12,055,190	0.2
OTHER DEPARTMENTAL EXPENSES	340,841,766	6.1
TOTAL DEPARTMENTAL EXPENSES	2,704,095,252	48.4
DEPARTMENTAL INCOME(- LOSS)	2,880,464,612	51.6

Source: *Nevada Gaming Abstract 1992*, State Gaming Control Board, (Carson City, NV 1993)

TABLE 5.4
PER SQUARE FOOT ANALYSIS AND RATIOS

Fiscal Year 1992
Statewide Casinos
With Gaming Revenue of $1,000,000 and over

AMOUNTS REPRESENT 192 LOCATION(S).

GAMING REVENUE PER SQUARE FOOT OF FLOOR SPACE

AREA	NO. OF CASINOS OPERATING	AVERAGE AREA IN SQUARE FEET	GAMING REVENUE PER SQUARE FOOT
PIT (INCLUDES BINGO AND KENO)	167	6,520	1,760
COIN OPERATED DEVICES	192	15,619	1,155
POKER AND PAN	73	1,082	946
RACE AND SPORTS	73	4,103	424
TOTAL CASINO	192	23,262	1,250

Source: *Nevada Gaming Abstract 1992*, State Gaming Control Board, (Carson City, NV 1993)

A Time of Major Changes

Traditionally, in addition to the opportunity to gamble, famous hotel/casinos like Caesars Palace, Circus World, the Dunes, the Golden Nugget, Harrah's, the Hilton, MGM Grand, and the Sahara offer a resort-type atmosphere, with big name entertainment, luxurious accommodations, and lavish restaurants. Some also feature jai-alai frontons, tennis, golf, swimming, and the occasional cattle auction.

Gambling is a business, just like selling cars, reference books, or corn flakes. While the handle in Nevada has continued to grow, there is no guarantee that demand may not slacken in the future. Furthermore, casinos outside of Nevada and Atlantic City, as small as some of them might be, offer another alternative to potential gamblers who might choose to visit Dubuque, Iowa, or a nearby Native-American reservation instead of flying all the way to Las Vegas.

As a result, Las Vegas is going through one of the most exciting times in the history of the entire gambling industry. While the 1980s were dominated by the spread of lotteries from coast to coast, gambling in the 1990s will be dominated by the growth of casino gambling on Native-American Reservations (see below) and the development of huge, mega-complexes in Las Vegas.

The image of Las Vegas has benefitted from the spread of gambling throughout the American society. About three-fourths of the states now operate lotteries. Casino gambling in one form or another is legal (although not necessarily operative) in 20 states and Puerto Rico. At one time, many Americans connected Las Vegas with organized crime — after all, it was the gangster "Bugsy" Siegel who built the first gambling casino. Until recently, Las Vegas had worked hard to escape this image. Over the past decade, as gambling has become common throughout the United States, and even sanctioned by government, it has tended to lose whatever criminal character that may have been attached to it.

While gambling is the basis of these giant casinos, it is only part of the total experience. These new complexes offer opportunities for the whole family. Las Vegas is no longer a place for mother

---

TABLE 5.5
RATE OF ROOM OCCUPANCY

Fiscal Year 1992
Statewide Casinos
With Gaming Revenue of $1,000,000 and over

AMOUNTS REPRESENT 192 LOCATION(S).

ROOMS: MONTH:	AVAILABLE ROOMS	ROOMS OCCUPIED	% OF OCCUPANCY (COMPUTED)
JULY	2,536,750	2,235,334	88.12
AUGUST	2,555,434	2,343,543	91.71
SEPTEMBER . . .	2,462,792	2,168,521	88.05
OCTOBER	2,541,803	2,299,707	90.48
NOVEMBER . . .	2,461,944	1,977,408	80.32
DECEMBER . . .	2,523,206	1,901,943	75.38
JANUARY	2,542,220	2,033,552	79.99
FEBRUARY . . .	2,407,202	2,124,148	88.24
MARCH	2,560,565	2,212,763	86.42
APRIL	2,468,024	2,191,989	88.82
MAY	2,571,198	2,285,866	88.90
JUNE	2,486,278	2,214,229	89.06
TOTAL	30,117,416	25,989,003	86.29

AVERAGE PIT REVENUE PER ROOM PER DAY	73.75	AVERAGE BEVERAGE SALES PER ROOM PER DAY	20.18
AVERAGE SLOT REVENUE PER ROOM PER DAY	133.24	AVERAGE ROOMS DEPARTMENT PAYROLL PER ROOM PER DAY	15.98
AVERAGE FOOD SALES PER ROOM PER DAY	42.39	AVERAGE ROOM RATE PER DAY	48.78

Source: *Nevada Gaming Abstract 1992*, State Gaming Control Board, (Carson City, NV 1993)

and father to go alone and gamble at the slot machines or casino tables — it is a complete attraction to which the whole family can come and enjoy themselves.

In 1989 and 1990, the huge, 3,000-room Mirage hotel and the even larger, 4,000-room Excalibur, the biggest hotel in the world, opened in Las Vegas. Rather than simply billing themselves as casinos, these two new, enormous hotels present themselves as resorts that happen to offer casinos as one form of entertainment.

The Mirage hotel has become a "must see" Polynesian-style attraction in the Nevada desert with a $13-million, erupting volcano outside and a 20,000-gallon aquarium filled with exotic tropical fish. The Excalibur presents itself as an idyllic medieval time. Medieval-costumed hosts greet arriving guests and telephone operators tell guests to "dave a royal day."

In 1993, three more gigantic hotels/casinos/tourist attractions opened up. The Luxor Las Vegas is a 30-story pyramid covered by 11 acres of glass. In front of the hotel is a huge obelisk and copy of the Sphynx. A Nile River flows inside the hotel and the atrium is the world's largest. The hotel's 2,526 rooms are done in an ancient Egyptian style. The casino covers more than 100,000 square feet.

In keeping with its efforts to attract families with children, the hotel contains a Sega amusement arcade and Sega has agreed to introduce all its new video products at the hotel before it markets them nationwide. In addition, Sega is opening VirtuaLand, a virtual reality facility of 20,000 square feet. A huge child care center allows parents to leave their children under adult supervision while they go off to play the slot machines or visit the roulette tables.

The Treasure Island Resort is based on Robert Louis Stevenson's classic tale of piracy. The three 36-story towers holding 2,900 rooms face onto Buccaneer Bay, a theme park designed to look like a seaport of the 1700s. Every hour two 90-foot frigates do battle. In addition, the hotel also offers video games and other electronically simulated games.

The MGM Grand Hotel is the largest hotel (5,005 rooms in four 30-story towers) and gambling casino (as big as four football fields) in the world. In front, a seven-story lion guards the hotel. The hotel contains a 33-acre theme park with 12 major attractions plus a giant swimming complex. While the Vegas World may have only "937" rooms, its owner Bob Stupak is constructing a 1,012 foot tower that will be even higher than the Eiffel Tower in Paris. On top of the tower will be a restaurant, two observation decks, and four suites with a view for the high rollers, bettors who wager large amounts of money.

These are some of the largest hotels in the world costing huge amounts of money. The Luxor cost an estimated $390 million, the Treasure Island $450 million, and the MGM Grand $1.03 billion. These investments will likely change the way the gambling business is done in Las Vegas. It may no longer be enough to offer only a hotel and gambling casino. Certainly that is what the owners of the five mega-hotels described above believe.

Since 1989 when the Mirage and Excalibur opened, five of the famous old-line casinos, including the Dunes and the Riviera, have gone bankrupt. While the new casinos hope to attract the many millions of Americans who have never visited Las Vegas (MGM Grand Chief Executive Robert Maxey claims that his studies show that only 15 percent of Americans have ever been to Las Vegas), it is likely that other casinos may not survive. On the other hand, many owners of the older casinos hope that the new influx of tourists will actually benefit them. In addition, as well as offering an alternative to the older gambling casinos, these new hotel/casinos offer an alternative to the family considering a trip to Disneyland in Anaheim, California or Disney World in Orlando, Florida.

Statistics

TABLE 5.6

CASINO INDUSTRY FACILITY
AT DECEMBER 1992 AND 1991

	Bally's Grand		Bally's Park Place		Caesars		Claridge		Harrah's Marina		Resorts	
	1992	1991	1992	1991	1992	1991	1992	1991	1992	1991	1992	1991
Table Games:												
Blackjack	53	59	60	70	54	52	44	43	60	76	56	60
Craps	14	18	14	18	16	20	10	10	14	16	12	16
Roulette	10	10	12	12	11	13	6	6	14	18	9	13
Big Six	3	3	3	4	2	2	1	1	1	2	2	4
Baccarat	1	2	2	2	3	3	0	1	1	1	2	2
Minibaccarat	3	2	2	2	3	2	3	1	1	3	2	2
Red Dog (a)	2	2	1	2	0	1	1	3	1	2	1	2
Sic Bo (b)	1	0	1	1	2	1	1	0	1	1	1	0
Pai Gow Poker (c)	2	0	2	0	4	0	1	0	4	0	2	0
Pokette (d)	0	0	0	0	0	0	0	0	0	0	0	0
Total Table Games	89	96	97	111	95	94	67	65	97	119	87	99
Slot Machines:												
.05 slot machines	33	69	75	92	0	91	68	69	0	94	34	85
.25 slot machines	818	730	1,084	1,004	957	928	946	943	1,105	953	1,060	1,037
.50 slot machines	261	240	302	268	174	196	79	92	284	294	265	237
$1 slot machines	279	272	357	329	545	487	225	263	467	476	331	288
$5 slot machines	49	43	65	71	84	55	13	6	61	47	42	35
$25 slot machines	7	7	10	10	17	15	1	1	2	2	5	5
$100 slot machines	2	2	4	4	13	16	0	0	2	1	1	1
Other slot machines (e)	0	0	0	0	15	11	0	0	0	0	0	0
Total Slot Machines	1,449	1,363	1,897	1,778	1,805	1,799	1,332	1,374	1,921	1,867	1,738	1,688
Casino Sq. Footage	45,442	45,442	64,435	64,410	60,000	60,000	43,579	43,579	61,183	61,278	60,000	60,000
Number of Hotel Rooms	518	518	1,269	1,267	641	649	501	501	760	760	669	671
Number of Parking Spaces	1,723	1,723	2,374	2,319	2,909	2,895	1,292	1,268	2,678	2,678	1,431	1,538
Fixed Asset Investment ($ in Millions) (f)	$311.8	$303.1	$741.8	$736.8	$411.3	$396.8	$13.6(g)	$13.9(g)	$364.9	$343.9	$178.1	$162.6
Number of Employees	3,003	3,025	3,868	3,929	3,479	3,957	2,373	2,190	3,458	3,432	3,893	4,004

(a) Red Dog was introduced on July 1, 1991
(b) Sic Bo was introduced on December 6, 1991
(c) Pai Gow Poker was introduced on May 12, 1992
(d) Pokette was introduced on June 25, 1992
(e) Includes all other slot machines
(f) Represents property and equipment before accumulated depreciation as reported by each casino licensee
(g) Fixed asset investment for Claridge at December 31, 1992 and 1991, only includes gaming equipment because
    The Claridge at Park Place, Incorporated leases its property and equipment as a result of a sale and refinancing agreement

(Continued on following page.)

TABLE 5.6 (Continued)

	Sands 1992	Sands 1991	Showboat 1992	Showboat 1991	TropWorld 1992	TropWorld 1991	Trump Castle 1992	Trump Castle 1991	Trump Plaza 1992	Trump Plaza 1991	Trump Taj Mahal 1992	Trump Taj Mahal 1991	Industry Totals 1992	Industry Totals 1991
	47	59	41	46	66	97	51	57	61	68	98	99	691	786
	14	17	12	16	16	20	16	17	9	16	22	30	169	214
	13	13	9	10	15	16	11	12	13	13	18	21	141	157
	1	3	1	1	2	3	2	2	2	3	6	6	26	34
	4	4	2	3	3	3	4	3	2	2	5	4	29	30
	2	2	2	2	2	2	3	2	4	3	2	2	29	25
	1	2	1	2	1	4	1	2	0	1	2	2	12	25
	1	0	0	0	1	1	1	1	2	1	1	1	13	7
	2	0	2	0	4	0	2	0	4	0	4	0	33	0
	0	0	0	0	1	0	0	0	0	0	0	0	1	0
	85	100	70	80	111	146	91	96	97	107	158	165	1,144	1,278
	0	71	94	96	0	122	74	85	48	84	156	158	582	1,116
	898	700	1,451	1,365	1,387	1,342	1,094	1,028	999	955	1,811	1,762	13,610	12,747
	265	259	183	137	354	358	232	158	239	227	312	305	2,950	2,771
	319	313	285	268	684	506	352	307	409	364	544	437	4,797	4,310
	62	46	20	20	89	87	42	40	56	30	79	64	662	544
	6	4	3	2	10	8	5	5	6	4	5	5	77	68
	3	3	2	2	4	4	2	2	4	2	3	3	40	40
	0	0	0	0	32	0	2	0	7	6	0	0	56	17
	1,553	1,396	2,038	1,890	2,560	2,427	1,803	1,625	1,768	1,672	2,910	2,734	22,774	21,613
	49,789	50,123	59,858	59,623	90,774	90,774	62,595	60,000	60,000	60,000	120,000	120,000	777,655	775,229
	534	500	516	516	1,021	1,019	725	703	557(i)	1,065	1,250	1,250	8,961	9,419
	2,081	2,081	2,534	2,534	3,342	3,324	2,816	2,816	2,773	2,773	4,320	4,320	30,273	30,269
	$303.8	$300.9	$298.7	$280.7	$325.4(h)	$320.6(h)	$483.1	$474.5	$409.7	$401.9	$846.6	$834.9	$4,688.8	$4,570.6
	3,278	3,407	3,671	3,601	4,440	4,381	3,081	3,590	3,705	3,860	5,991	5,576	44,240	44,952

(h) Fixed asset investment for TropWorld at December 31, 1992 and 1991 does not include the original building and certain non-gaming assets because Adamar of New Jersey, Inc. leases these assets as a result of a sale and leaseback transaction
(i) Number of hotel rooms for Trump Plaza decreased by 500 because as of October 1, 1992, they do not lease Trump Regency

Source: *Casino Control Commission 1992 Annual Report*, Trenton, NJ

47

All 12 casinos operating in Atlantic City in 1992 were of the hotel/casino variety. (Table 5.6 shows facility statistics.) Together, the casinos grossed $3.2 billion in 1992. Gross revenue and related taxes for each facility are shown in Table 5.7. As seen in Figure 5.1, Donald Trump's huge Taj Mahal has, by far, the largest market share of all the hotel/casinos in Atlantic City followed by Caesars' and TropWorld.

The 25-cent slot machines accounted for the largest casino win by game in 1992, followed by $1.00 and $.50 slot machines (Figure 5.2). Blackjack was the most profitable table game followed by craps. The market share of casino win by percentage for 1991 and 1992 is shown in Figure 5.2.

TABLE 5.7
THE NEW JERSEY CASINO INDUSTRY
GROSS REVENUE AND RELATED TAX
FOR THE YEARS ENDED DECEMBER 31, 1992 AND 1991
(\$ in Thousands)

Casino Hotel	Casino Win	Daily Average Casino Win	Adjustment for Uncollectibles	Gross Revenue	Tax
Bally's Grand					
1992	199,774	546	147	199,627	15,970
1991	191,490	525	1,549	189,941	15,195
Bally's Park Place					
1992	280,535	766	653	279,882	22,391
1991	267,141	732	1,352	265,788	21,263
Caesars					
1992	332,495	908	2,684	329,812	26,385
1991	309,094	847	5,296	303,799	24,304
Claridge					
1992	146,358	400	484	145,873	11,670
1991	135,406	371	530	134,875	10,790
Harrah's Marina					
1992	287,495	786	1,521	285,974	22,878
1991	283,912	778	1,921	281,991	22,559
Resorts					
1992	235,515	643	1,334	234,181	18,734
1991	220,127	603	3,077	217,050	17,364
Sands					
1992	245,230	670	2,962	242,268	19,381
1991	242,011	663	4,447	237,564	19,005
Showboat					
1992	257,703	704	1,162	256,541	20,523
1991	239,801	657	2,363	237,437	18,995
TropWorld					
1992	310,199	848	519	309,680	24,774
1991	287,026	786	1,787	285,239	22,819
Trump Castle					
1992	240,354	657	2,030	238,325	19,066
1991	196,493	538	2,997	193,496	15,480
Trump Plaza					
1992	264,251	722	4,933	259,318	20,745
1991	235,033	644	4,638	230,395	18,432
Trump Taj Mahal					
1992	416,060	1,137	6,041	410,019	32,802
1991	384,028	1,052	8,437	375,591	30,047

Source: *Casino Control Commission 1992 Annual Report*, Trenton, NJ

THE STATE OF NEW JERSEY CASINO CONTROL FUND

When the New Jersey legislature implemented legalized gambling in New Jersey, it established the Casino Revenue Fund to finance assistance programs for New Jersey's elderly and disabled. To finance the fund, the 12 operating casinos are taxed 8 percent of their gross revenues or "win" each month. In 1992, the fund collected $247 million. To be eligible for the programs supported by the Casino Revenue Fund, a person must be at least 65 years old or receiving Social Security disability benefits. The maximum income limit is $13,650 for single persons and $16,750 for married couples. The largest expenditure from the fund was $124.5 million to help people pay for medicine, followed closely by $118.9 million for general medical ser-

FIGURE 5.1

Market Share of Casino Win

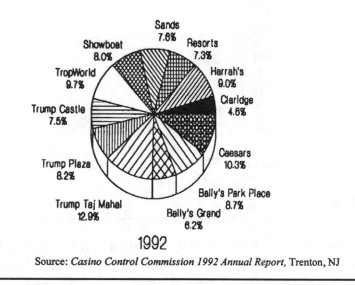

1992

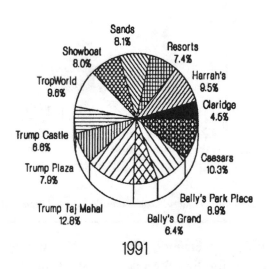

1991

Source: *Casino Control Commission 1992 Annual Report*, Trenton, NJ

vices. (See Figure 5.3 for a breakdown on how the Casino Revenue Fund was allotted. The $368.3 million in total expenditures in Figure 5.3 includes monies from a surplus of money already in the Casino Revenue Fund.)

Although income was up in 1992 for all New Jersey casinos, allowing them to recover from some recently shaky years, the future does not necessarily look bright. The New Jersey hotel/casinos basically offer gambling with attractions such as boxing matches or well-known entertainers. They do not, and probably cannot, offer the additional entertainment that the new hotel/casinos in Las Vegas are able to offer (see above). Furthermore, the city, which surrounds the Atlantic City gambling casinos, is dreary and rundown and is unlikely ever to become an added attraction to gamblers.

As noted in the 1992 *Annual Report of the New Jersey Casino Control Commission*,

Despite this steady climb [in revenues], state and local officials are no longer so sanguine about the notion that

such growth is inevitable. Atlantic City which long had a monopoly on casino gambling in the eastern half of the United States, now faces competition for that gaming dollar. From an Indian reservation in Connecticut to riverboats on the Mississippi, gamblers now have more options. And, with the likely prospect that even more jurisdictions will legalize casino gambling in coming years, that trend will only accelerate.

In response to this concern, Steven Perskie, the current Chairman of the Casino Control Commission, has brought a less adversarial relationship than had previously existed between the Casino Control Commission and the gambling industry in Atlantic City and has been able to introduce several major changes that have improved the financial situation of the casinos. Gambling can now take place 24 hours a day. More space can be used for casinos and more of that space can be used for more financially profitable slot machines. More and different types of games have been allowed. Simulcasting of horse races are now shown in the

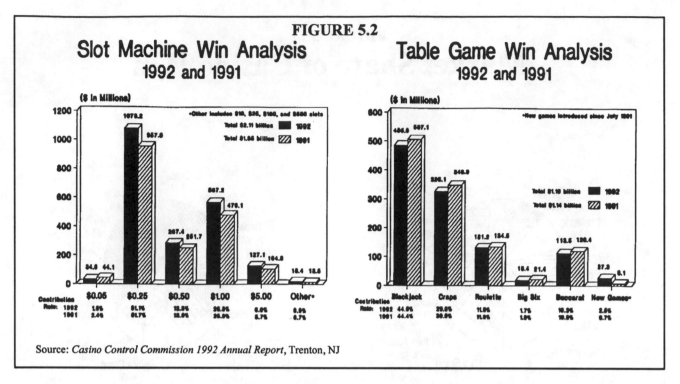

FIGURE 5.2

Slot Machine Win Analysis
1992 and 1991

Table Game Win Analysis
1992 and 1991

Source: *Casino Control Commission 1992 Annual Report*, Trenton, NJ

Atlantic City casinos. The state of New Jersey has provided funding for a new convention center and an expansion of the airport.

Nonetheless, according to the industry newsletter, *Atlantic City Action*, bus traffic, the major source of gamblers into Atlantic City, dropped 10 percent in 1993. The new gambling casino opened in Ledyard, Connecticut in 1992 by the Mashantucket Pequot (see below) has definitely cut into the number of visitors to Atlantic City. For New Englanders it is much easier to go to Ledyard than it is to travel all the way to Atlantic City. This is particularly important because most people who go to Atlantic City are day visitors who do not stay overnight. Saving three or four hours means more time to have fun, less time spent driving, and a chance to get home earlier. In addition, the opening of the new 90,000-square-foot casino on the Oneida Reservation near Verona, New York may take away many customers drawn from upstate New York. Finally, nearby Philadelphia, Pennsylvania is considering introducing casino gambling. Should the city decide to do so, it could be disastrous to Atlantic City.

EMPLOYMENT

The gambling industry is the major employer in Nevada, with the 192 major casinos employing

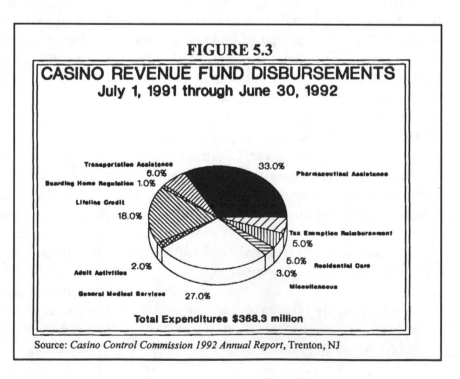

FIGURE 5.3

CASINO REVENUE FUND DISBURSEMENTS
July 1, 1991 through June 30, 1992

Total Expenditures $368.3 million

Source: *Casino Control Commission 1992 Annual Report*, Trenton, NJ

almost 156,000 Nevada residents in 1992 (Table 5.8). Gamblers may tip casino employees, but all tips are pooled and divided equally among the employees to prevent any collusion between employees and customers. Many workers in the larger casinos earn more in tips than they do from their base salaries.

In New Jersey, the casino industry employed 44,952 full-time people in 1992 and had a total annual payroll of about $920 million. About half (52 percent) worked in the hotel section, while 42 percent worked in the casinos (Figures 5.4). The majority of these employees did not live in Atlantic City, but commuted to work from other nearby cities (Figure 5.5).

PROMOTING GAMBLING

The largest expenditure for any casino is the cost of promoting itself. These outlays include direct advertising and promotion, as well as the junket and complimentary expenses (which can include free airline tickets, lodging, food, and drinks). Complimentary flights and rooms offered to preferred customers, the so-called "high-rollers," usually account for about 10 to 15 percent of the larger hotels' budgets.

Junkets, where a hotel/casino offers complimentary transportation, room, food, and drinks to groups of eight or more people, can be very risky for the casino, as each customer must gamble at least $2,500 in order for the hotel to cover the costs of accommodating the junketeers. Of the total expenses incurred by the major casinos in Nevada in 1992, 17 percent of room expenses, 19 percent of food expenses, and 57 percent of beverage expenses were complimentary. Both junketeers and complimentary visitors who do not gamble enough to provide the hotel with a profit are usually not invited to return.

In order to get and hold the "high-rollers," many casinos are introducing special programs similar to the airline mileage programs. Individu-

TABLE 5.8	
AVERAGE NUMBER OF EMPLOYEES FOR THE YEAR	
CASINO DEPARTMENT	53,052
ROOMS DEPARTMENT	20,882
FOOD DEPARTMENT	37,297
BEVERAGE DEPARTMENT	11,364
G & A DEPARTMENT	26,051
OTHER DEPARTMENTS	7,316
TOTAL	155,962

Source: *Nevada Gaming Abstract 1992*, State Gaming Control Board, (Carson City, NV 1993)

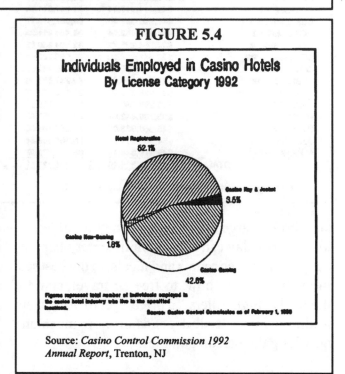

FIGURE 5.4

Source: *Casino Control Commission 1992 Annual Report*, Trenton, NJ

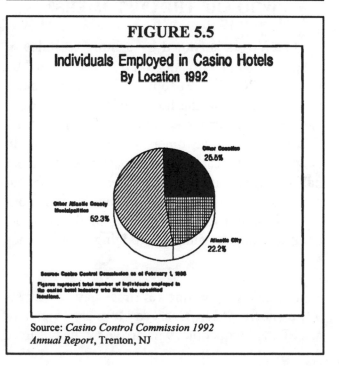

FIGURE 5.5

Source: *Casino Control Commission 1992 Annual Report*, Trenton, NJ

51

TABLE 5.9
SOUTH DAKOTA COMMISSION ON GAMING
GROSS REVENUE TAX SUMMARY
SINCE GAMING BEGAN IN NOV. 1989

	TOTAL GAMING ACTION	TOTAL GROSS REVENUES	8% GAMING TAX	(40%) STATE OF S.D.	(10%) LAWRENCE COUNTY	(50%) COMMISSION FUND
FY '90 (11/89–6/90)	$145,444,096.71	$14,330,125.35	$1,116,222.28	$446,488.91	$111,622.23	$558,111.14
FY '91 (07/90–06/91)	$329,967,978.96	$33,070,870.23	$2,605,325.94	$1,042,130.38	$260,532.59	$1,302,662.97
FY '92 (07/91–06/92)	$389,440,596.17	$38,619,946.28	$3,044,576.95	$1,217,830.78	$304,457.70	$1,522,288.48
JULY '92	$52,228,309.15	$5,235,343.37	$413,021.21	$165,208.48	$41,302.12	$206,510.61
AUGUST '92	$45,414,340.44	$4,641,211.58	$366,357.82	$146,543.13	$36,635.78	$183,178.91
SEPTEMBER '92	$45,248,397.55	$4,667,475.77	$367,644.39	$147,057.76	$36,764.44	$183,822.20
OCTOBER '92	$34,821,562.04	$3,484,911.23	$274,966.45	$109,986.58	$27,496.65	$137,483.23
NOVEMBER '92	$24,354,225.72	$2,404,650.63	$187,928.57	$75,171.43	$18,792.86	$93,964.29
DECEMBER '92	$20,641,957.15	$2,063,769.68	$159,829.24	$63,931.70	$15,982.92	$79,914.62
JANUARY '93	$24,144,526.45	$2,486,767.82	$192,315.18	$76,926.07	$19,231.52	$96,157.59
FEBRUARY '93	$26,718,646.39	$2,797,582.48	$213,280.38	$85,312.15	$21,328.04	$106,640.19
MARCH '93	$33,228,673.90	$3,310,936.75	$256,053.45	$102,421.38	$25,605.35	$128,026.73
APRIL '93	$30,293,940.70	$3,126,726.28	$245,240.00	$98,096.00	$24,524.00	$122,620.00
MAY '93	$35,709,442.94	$3,530,757.42	$272,895.58	$109,158.23	$27,289.56	$136,447.79
JUNE '93	$45,068,983.00	$4,258,186.03	$331,764.75	$132,705.90	$33,176.48	$165,882.38
JULY '93	$54,900,981.74	$5,368,889.34	$418,734.22	$167,493.69	$41,873.42	$209,367.11
AUGUST '93	$49,976,845.15	$5,103,272.97	$398,189.73	$159,275.89	$39,818.97	$199,094.87
TOTAL:	$1,387,603,306.16	$138,441,425.01	$10,864,346.14	$4,345,738.46	$1,086,434.61	$5,432,173.07

Source: South Dakota Commission on Gaming, Pierre, SD

als who bet large amounts of money for at least 3 to 4 hours a day can earn complimentary benefits ranging from free rooms and meals, to the best seat in the house at a show, to free air travel, and, for the really "high rollers," a private jet to bring them to the casinos. It all depends on how much and how long the person gambles.

WHO ARE THE CUSTOMERS?

Las Vegas is ringed by a hundred miles of desert. Atlantic City sits in an area inhabited by well over 20 million people. The Super Casinos in Las Vegas and the hotel/casino complexes in New Jersey offer the same type of gambling activities, but their customers are very different. In Nevada, the typical gambler can afford to fly (about half fly in) or drive long distances to reach the casinos. A trip to Las Vegas or Reno is often considered a major vacation, combining the elements of entertainment with plush lodgings and a chance to get rich.

Atlantic City casino revenues have traditionally come from "East Coast day-trippers," individuals, often older people, who arrive by the bus from nearby metropolitan areas such as New York City or Philadelphia. (While Atlantic City is making greater use of its airport, only about 5 percent of visitors fly in.) Bus trips are often arranged by tour agencies, some of whom are associated with the casinos. The "day-tripper" pays for a package tour which might include a meal and some small amount of money to be used at the gaming tables or slot machines. "Day-trippers" do not usually have as much money to spend as visitors to Las Vegas or Reno, and, therefore, generally produce much less revenue for the casinos. As their name implies, they do not stay overnight at the hotels.

CASINO GAMBLING SPREADS
ACROSS THE COUNTRY

Recreating the Old West

As many areas of the Midwest and West began to suffer from a changing and often declining economy, some states and localities began to look for alternative ways to raise money and attract tourists. The voters of South Dakota approved casino gambling in the town of Deadwood, where Wild Bill Hickock was killed. The town has been transformed into a gambling center. While promoters of the casino gambling expected gamblers to bet around $4 million the first year, they bet over $145 million. This figure more than doubled to $330 million in FY 1991 and action reached $389.4 million for FY 1992.

Meanwhile, revenues for the South Dakota gambling casinos rose from $14.3 million in FY 1990 to $33 million in FY 1991 and $38.6 million in FY 1992 (Table 5.9). The government collected an 8 percent tax on the revenues. The overwhelming majority of revenues (88 percent) was produced by the slot machines, mostly the 25 cent machines which produced 63 percent of all slot machine revenues. (See Table 5.10 for August 1993 monthly summary.)

TABLE 5.10
SOUTH DAKOTA GAMING STATISTICS
MONTHLY SUMMARY
AUGUST 1993

SLOT MACHINES

	NUMBER OF UNITS	COINS IN	GROSS REVENUES	AVERAGE HOLD %	AVG. DAILY HOLD/UNIT
$1.00	220	$9,878,594.90	$824,872.23	8.35%	$120.95
$0.50	6	$77,267.50	$7,180.85	9.29%	$38.61
$0.25	1182	$28,619,915.90	$2,808,146.94	9.81%	$76.64
$0.10	17	$301,119.30	$33,124.20	11.00%	$62.85
$0.05	594	$6,988,697.80	$802,287.98	11.48%	$43.57
TOTALS:	2019	$45,865,595.40	$4,475,612.20	9.76%	$71.51

CARD GAMES

	NUMBER OF TABLES	DROP	GROSS REVENUES	AVERAGE HOLD %	AVG. DAILY HOLD/UNIT
BLACK JACK	62	$2,204,209.75	$436,976.77	19.82%	$227.36
POKER	18	$190,684.00	$190,684.00		$341.73
TOTALS:	80	$2,394,893.75	$627,660.77		$253.09

TOTAL GROSS REVENUE:	$5,103,272.97
LESS CITY SLOTS:	$129,479.68
ADJUSTED GROSS REVENUES:	$4,973,793.29
	* 8%
TAX DUE:	$397,903.46
ADJUSTMENTS:	$286.27
TAX COLLECTED IN AUGUST:	$398,189.73

TAX ALLOCATIONS

TOTAL 8% TAX:	$398,189.73
LESS:STATE (40%)	$159,275.89
LESS:LAWRENCE CO. (10%)	$39,818.97
EQUALS:COMMISSION SHARE	$199,094.87
PLUS:CITY SLOTS REVENUE	$36,490.90
TOTAL TO COMMISSION FUND:	$235,585.77

TOTAL GAMING ACTION

SLOT MACHINES	$45,865,595.40
CARD GAMES	$4,111,049.75
	$49,976,645.15
OVERALL HOLD PERCENTAGE:	10.21%

Source: South Dakota Commission on Gaming, Pierre, SD

Meanwhile in Colorado, casinos are springing up in the historic mining towns of Central City, Black Hawk, and Cripple Creek. Single bets in both South Dakota and Colorado are limited to $5.00, but at $5.00 a throw, large amounts of money can still be lost rather quickly. In FY 1993, 69 casinos were operating in Colorado, double the 35 operating in FY 1992. These casinos produced $226,528,923 in revenues, more than double the $96,318,657 of the year before. The number of gambling devices went from 3,591 in FY 1992 to 10,838 in FY 1993. In FY 1993, Black Hawk had 20 casinos producing $84.6 million in revenues, Central City had 21 casinos producing $79.3 million in revenues, and Cripple Creek had 29 casinos producing $62.6 million in revenues.

The State of Colorado taxes at 2 percent of the first million and 20 percent thereafter. In FY 1992, the state collected $10,792,403, and in FY 1993 it took in $30,126,720. Just under half (46 percent) went to the State General Fund, about one-fourth (28 percent) went to the State Historical Fund, and most of the rest went to the three gambling towns and the counties they were in. (See Figure 5.6.)

While there has been some turnover in the casinos in South Dakota and Colorado, a rather nor-

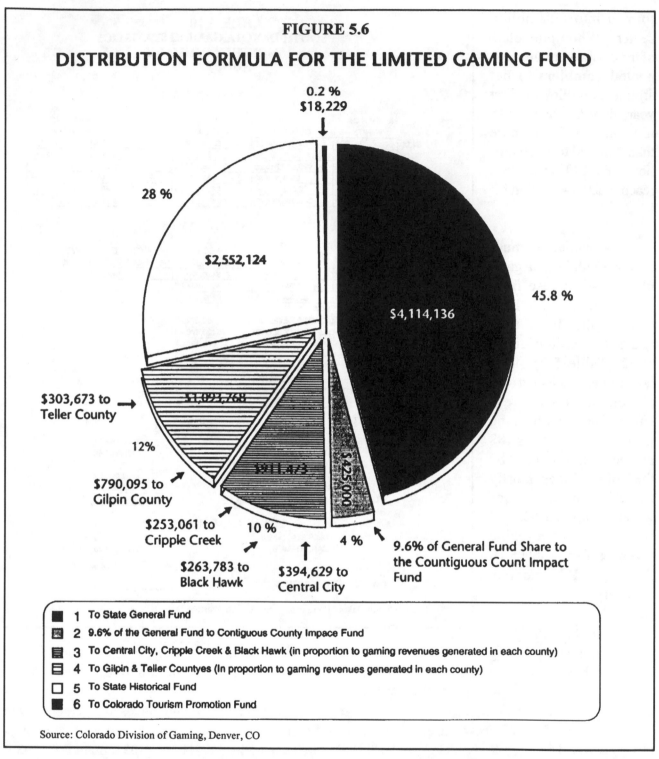

FIGURE 5.6

DISTRIBUTION FORMULA FOR THE LIMITED GAMING FUND

0.2 %
$18,229

28 %

$2,552,124

45.8 %

$4,114,136

$303,673 to
Teller County

$1,093,768

12%

$790,095 to
Gilpin County

$911,473

$425,000

$253,061 to
Cripple Creek

10 %

4 %

9.6% of General Fund Share to
the Countiguous Count Impact
Fund

$263,783 to
Black Hawk

$394,629 to
Central City

■	1	To State General Fund
▨	2	9.6% of the General Fund to Contiguous County Impace Fund
▤	3	To Central City, Cripple Creek & Black Hawk (in proportion to gaming revenues generated in each county)
▥	4	To Gilpin & Teller Countyes (In proportion to gaming revenues generated in each county)
☐	5	To State Historical Fund
■	6	To Colorado Tourism Promotion Fund

Source: Colorado Division of Gaming, Denver, CO

mal occurrence in any new area of business as large number of entrepreneurs, many of them inexperienced, scramble for a piece of the action, there is little question that gambling is here to stay in the historic mining towns. Meanwhile, in the East, people living near the oceanside counties in Maryland can play the slot machines with a percentage of the winnings going to charity.

Riverboat Gambling

Several states that forbid casino gambling on dry land take a kinder view of gambling on water. On April 1, 1991, the state of Iowa brought back riverboat gambling to the Mississippi River. Since then five more states (MO, IL, IN, MS, and LA) have passed laws permitting riverboat casinos. As

54

of November 1993, 22 riverboats (3 in Iowa, 9 in Illinois, and 10 in Mississippi) were sailing out onto rivers so that their guests could play the slot machines or the casino tables. Another 29 ships (1 for a company in Iowa, 3 for Illinois, 14 for Mississippi, 7 for Louisiana, and 4 for Missouri) are under construction. At least another 52 are in the planning stage.

Most of these riverboats range in size from 200 to 300 feet long and 45 to 95 feet wide. The *President* sailing out of Davenport, Iowa, is 300 feet long has a casino of 27,000 square feet, 669 slot machines and 38 gaming tables. The smaller *Par-A-Dice* out of Peoria, Illinois, is 228 feet long, has 12,500 square feet of casino space with 478 slot machines and 40 tables.

Not all the riverboats must be seaworthy. Iowa and Illinois demand that the riverboats cruise in the rivers, while Missouri and Louisiana require the ships to cruise to an ill-defined "certain extent." Mississippi and Louisiana do not require the ships to sail and, in fact, many of the ships docked in Mississippi are not really capable of sailing — they are giant buildings constructed on barges.

Betting losses on the Iowa riverboats are limited to $200 per cruise. The gambler buys up to $200 worth of scrip before getting on board. When the bettor gets on board, he or she can then change the scrip into tokens or chips for gambling. If a player takes four cruises in one day, he or she can lose up to $800. If someone simply wants to enjoy a brief cruise on the Mississippi and not bet money, he or she can usually buy a cruise-only ticket for $10 or less. The $200 limit, however, has led many riverboat casinos to sail for more profitable shores. For example, the *Diamond Lady* and the *Emerald Lady* steamed to Mississippi, and some observers fear for the future of riverboat gambling in Iowa if the limit is maintained.

Meanwhile, across the river in Illinois, gamblers have the opportunity to bet without limit. Illinois believes that gamblers will come to their state instead of Iowa because of this policy. Missouri, across the river from Illinois and, now considering applications for riverboats licenses, has a $500 loss limit.

Farther down the river, Mississippi legalized gambling in 1990 and already 10 riverboats are steaming out of Mississippi ports. Biloxi alone has four ships in port and another four are expected soon. Louisiana approved riverboat gambling in 1991. The new law will allow 15 riverboats on the 11 rivers and lakes. While the law limits the number of riverboats per parish (county) to six, most of the riverboats will likely sail out of New Orleans or nearby parishes. The New Orleans metropolitan area spreads out over Orleans, Jefferson, St. Tammany, and St. Bernard parishes, so it is possible that all 15 riverboats could serve the New Orleans region.

With a few exceptions (mainly video poker, which limits bets to $2.00 and jackpots to $500), there will be no limits on betting or losses. Betting on horseracing (off-track betting) will be permitted. There will be no limit on the number of cruises a riverboat can make in a day. Seven boats are already under construction. These riverboats will be much larger than those plying the Mississippi River near Iowa or Illinois, measuring over 300 feet long and holding 2,500 to 3,000 passengers.

Many state political leaders and residents believe that riverboat gambling will turn around Louisiana's seriously ailing economy and perhaps transform the city into the next Las Vegas. A Louisiana State University study concluded that riverboat gambling would bring an additional 550,000 visitors to New Orleans every year, increase annual income by almost $300 million and contribute an additional $85 million to city and state treasuries.

According to Eugene Martin Christiansen, in his annual report on the industry published in *Gambling and Wagering Business*, gamblers on boats based in Iowa, Illinois, and Mississippi bet nearly $7.3 billion in 1992, almost 7 times the $1.1 billion they wagered in 1991. Revenues totalled $418 million in 1992.

Some observers believe riverboat gambling is only a transitional step toward eventual land-based gambling. Nonetheless, other states such as West Virginia and Pennsylvania and the City of Chicago (which is presently the only area of Illinois not permitted riverboats) have been considering riverboats. On the other hand, Alabama, Kansas, Kentucky, and Wisconsin have rejected the idea. In these states, land-based casinos, or factions supporting the eventual development of land-based casinos, were able to help defeat the proposal. There can be little question, however, that many politicians and other leaders in these states prefer land-based casinos to riverboats. Nonetheless, by 1995, an estimated 60 riverboats are expected to be active on the nation's waterways.

Other Places to Gamble on the Water

Regular Cruises

Virtually all major cruise lines include gambling as an attraction for their passengers along with entertainment, dining, dancing, and shuffleboard. The Carnival Cruise Lines' *Ecstasy*, a particularly large cruise ship, has 234 slots, 16 blackjack tables, 3 roulette wheels, 2 crap tables, and 3 Caribbean stud poker tables. The cruise lines emphasize that gambling is just one among many attractions. They further stress that they are a hospitality business, not a gambling business.

Virtually all cruise passengers are there to enjoy the cruise experience, not to gamble. As a result, most cruise ships have a limit of $100 to 200 in order to control losses. After all, a cruise passenger will not have had a pleasant voyage if she or he lost huge amounts of money at the gaming tables. *Gaming and Wagering Business* estimates that cruise casinos handled $4.3 billion in 1992, better than three times the estimated $1.8 billion in 1990. Many cruise lines are now introducing lotteries into their gaming programs.

Card Rooms

Cardrooms are small gambling parlors where individuals can come to play cards, usually poker and blackjack, with other people for money. The parlor usually earns its revenues by charging the players for every hour or every hand they play. Currently, card rooms are legal, although not necessarily operative, in 14 states. Public cardrooms have been legal in California since the Gold Rush days. Currently over 300 licensed gambling parlors with over 2,000 tables are operating in California. While card games have always been part of the state's western tradition, the passing of Proposition 13 limiting property taxes left many cities and counties in difficult financial straits. As a result, cities like Bell Gardens, Commerce, and Huntington Park legalized card clubs in an effort to raise revenue.

Traditionally, card clubs had been small establishments, but some of the more recently developed clubs have been considerably larger. The largest card club in California is the Bicycle Club in Bell Gardens with 170 tables which generates $10 million a year for the city, about 60 percent of Bell Garden's municipal budget. Every day 5,000 to 7,000 players play poker at the Bicycle Club wagering an estimated $1 billion a year.

Card clubs in California got another boost from the introduction of games of Asian origin, often called the "Asian Games." Games such as Pai Gow and Super Pan Nine are much faster, and for many people, more exciting. With the introduction of these games, more people have begun visiting these card rooms and have given the industry a real boost.

The State of Washington has more than 80 clubs and limits bets to $10 per bet. Montana has over 50 small clubs and limits the action to $300 per pot. North Dakota has about 20 clubs, with most of the proceeds going to charity. While these small clubs provide a source of revenue for the operators, they often provide a social setting for the players. The players often know each other

FIGURE 5.7

How America Feels About Casino Gaming

Acceptance of Casino Gaming

There is a high level of acceptance of casino gaming as a behavior among Americans.

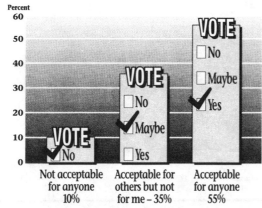

Not acceptable
for anyone
10%

Acceptable for
others but not
for me – 35%

Acceptable
for anyone
55%

Source: Harrah's / YCS Monitor

ACCEPTANCE OF GAMING	
	PERCENTAGE OF U.S.
Perfectly acceptable for anyone	55%
Acceptable for others, but not for me	35%
Not acceptable for anyone	10%
	100%

Source: *The Harrah's Survey of U.S. Casino Gaming Entertainment*, Harrah's Casino Hotels, (Memphis, TN 1993)

and look upon playing poker as a form of recreation and a chance to get together with friends and acquaintances. Players know there will always be a game going on down at the local card room. Oregon permits "social gambling" — small-stakes poker and blackjack — in taverns and bars. As noted above, cardrooms can also be found in Deadwood, South Dakota, and in Central City, Black Hawk, and Cripple Creek, Colorado.

While card tables are available in Nevada and Atlantic City, casino operators do not see them as very profitable. In Nevada, the house take is limited to about 2.5 percent of the pot. Consequently, the per-square-foot income does not come near the output of other types of gambling. As a result, the casinos in Las Vegas have only about 300 tables and there are only about 500 tables in all of Nevada. In 1992, the 192 casinos in Nevada brought in only $78 million from cardrooms, barely 1.4 percent of the casinos' revenues. In New Jersey a whole host of newly-permitted table games, including the Asian games of Sic Bo and Pai Gow Poker, brought in about 2.5 percent of revenue. Generally, the big casinos look upon card games as a method of attracting gamblers to other games.

According to Eugene Christiansen, in his annual report prepared for *Gaming & Wagering Business*, over the past decade, betting in card rooms has increased more than eight-fold from an estimated $1 million in 1982 to an estimated $8.4 million in 1992. Most of it, an estimated $7.5 to $8.0 billion, was bet in California's 300 card rooms. Over the same period, revenues grew from $50 million to $661 million. (Figures for card rooms are only estimates since these rooms are privately-owned and need not report their earnings.)

The rapid growth in card games seems to have levelled off with little increase in handle or revenue from 1991 to 1992. Some observers believe that the market may have become saturated and will likely not grow much more.

GAMBLING ON NATIVE AMERICAN RESERVATIONS

As discussed in Chapter II, the Indian Gaming Regulatory Act (PL 100-497) permits Native-American tribes to introduce gambling on their reservations. Many tribes had already been holding bingo games on their reservations, but the new law opened up the possibility that other forms of gambling could be played on Native American lands. It also meant that the Native American tribes could play a major role in the large expansion of gambling occurring throughout the country.

While returns from bingo, the major form of gambling that was being played on reservations, were beginning to level off, many Native American tribes recognized casino games were being offered in more places throughout the United States. (See Chapter III.) They saw this as an opportunity to bring some prosperity to their reservations.

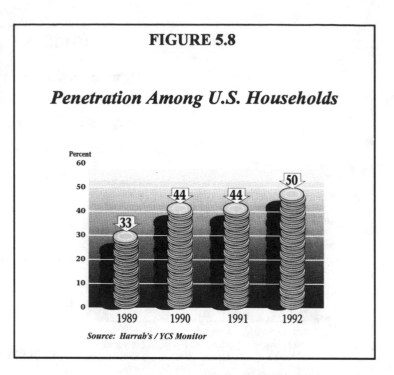

FIGURE 5.8

Penetration Among U.S. Households

Source: Harrah's / YCS Monitor

A New Opportuniity

The Indian Gaming Regulatory Act permitted the tribes to conduct any type of gambling on their reservation which was permitted in the state within which the reservation was located. The law also called for the tribe and the state to negotiate agreements or "compacts" which would allow this gambling. These compacts could permit types of gambling to take place on reservations that were not permitted in the state. The state was required to bargain with the tribes in good faith. If they did not, or if the tribe was not satisfied with the process, the law permitted the tribe to take the issue to court, an option that has been frequently used.

The amount of money bet on Native American reservations has risen from nothing in 1982 to an estimated $15 billion in 1992. The casino retained about 10 percent of the handle, for an estimated $1.5 billion in 1992.* Of this total, the tribes get a minimum of 60 percent or about $900 million. (The other $600 million went to the individuals or companies operating the casinos.) Gambling revenue from reservations has been increasing dramatically with income more than doubling from 1991 alone. In all likelihood, these numbers will continue to increase dramatically.

A Growing Number of Casinos

As of November 1993, according to the Bureau of Indian Affairs, 78 tribes in 18 states had negotiated compacts which permit casino gambling, a trend likely to increase. In Minnesota, 11 tribal compacts have led to the development of 14 high-stakes casinos. The Mille Lacs band of Chippewa Indians, for example, has built a $25 million casino gambling complex near Hinckley, Minnesota, with a 102,000 square foot casino containing 1,000 to 1,500 video slot machines, 60 blackjack tables, a 500-seat bingo hall, and a 100-150-seat keno hall.

---

* Of this amount, about $1.1 billion came from casino gambling and about $429 million came from bingo. In this particular case, the earnings are handled together because the most frequently asked question is how much money is being earned by Native Americans from gambling. It is important to remember that a significant proportion of Native American gambling revenues are being earned from bingo, although this proportion will decline significantly in the future.

In Colorado, the Southern Utes tribe and the Mountain Utes tribe both plan to open casinos. In the State of Washington, the Tulalip tribe has reached an agreement with the state eventually permitting 31 gaming tables with $10 and $20 bets. In Wisconsin, 11 tribes have reached agreement with the state to offer blackjack and electronic games of chance.

The Winnebago tribe plans to spend $17 million to expand its existing casino so that it will hold 1,000 slot machines and 40 blackjack tables. In San Diego, California, the 95-member Sycuan tribe has opened a $3 million, 58,000 square foot casino offering poker, bingo, off-track-betting, and lottery-type games on their reservation. In South Dakota, the Santee Sioux tribe runs a complete gambling hall. In Louisiana, the Tunica-Biloxi tribe plans to build a $25 million casino while the Coushatta tribe plans to construct a $35 million facility.

In upstate New York near Verona, the Oneida tribe opened a new 90,000-square-foot casino expected to serve 7,000 patrons a day around the clock. The Oneidas' plan to expand its offerings significantly in the near future. After a lengthy and heated battle with the state, the Mashantucket-Pequot tribe won a court order to be allowed to open a casino in Ledyard, in southeastern Connecticut. The 79,000-square-foot building offers gamblers blackjack, roulette, the big-six money wheel, baccarat, poker, and electronic video games. The casino has been so successful that dealers must work double shifts and lines form to play the games. Meanwhile, down the Atlantic Coast, in Atlantic City, New Jersey, casino operators are very concerned that the new gambling facility in Connecticut will draw customers away from the already ailing casinos in Atlantic City.

Gaming on reservations has not developed as rapidly in Canada. Despite efforts in British Columbia, Manitoba, New Brunswick, Ontario, and Saskatchewan, only Manitoba permits gambling on reservations, and this is limited to bingo, lotteries, and video lotteries. The provinces and the

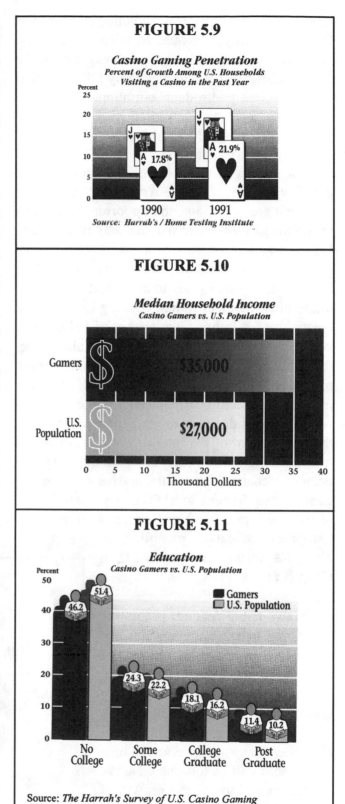

FIGURE 5.9

Casino Gaming Penetration
Percent of Growth Among U.S. Households
Visiting a Casino in the Past Year

1990: 17.8% 1991: 21.9%

Source: Harrah's / Home Testing Institute

FIGURE 5.10

Median Household Income
Casino Gamers vs. U.S. Population

Gamers: $35,000
U.S. Population: $27,000

Thousand Dollars

FIGURE 5.11

Education
Casino Gamers vs. U.S. Population

Gamers / U.S. Population

No College: 46.2 / 51.4
Some College: 24.3 / 22.2
College Graduate: 18.1 / 16.2
Post Graduate: 11.4 / 10.2

Source: *The Harrah's Survey of U.S. Casino Gaming Entertainment*, Harrah's Casino Hotels, (Memphis, TN 1993)

Native American tribes are battling over sovereignty. Many tribal leaders believe they are sovereign nations and do not have to reach an agreement with the province in which their reservation

59

is located. Other tribal leaders believe that despite their sovereignty, it would be wiser to reach an agreement and avoid the pain and expense of the long legal battle that will inevitably follow should they unilaterally introduce gambling.

A Few Problems

The Indian Gaming Act of 1988 has given a growing number of Native-American tribes, many of which are very poor, the opportunity to "cash in" on the gambling boom of the last several years. Like any new business venture, the budding tribal gambling establishments have run into some problems. It took three years to appoint the members to the three-member Indian Gaming Commission created by the Indian Gaming Act of 1988 which was supposed to develop the policies and procedures necessary to develop the tribal gaming projects. Gambling frequently attracts disreputable individuals and some tribal leaders have made unwise financial deals. A recent report prepared by the Department of the Interior noted a number of tribes had signed contracts in which the tribes had been overcharged for administrative services and gambling equipment. In addition, several bills have already been presented in Congress to limit the development of casino gambling on Native-America reservations. (See Chapter II.)

Many tribal leaders recognize that some tribal managers may be victimized or may expand beyond their ability to handle their growth. Nonetheless, they note, these are typical business problems that often develop in a new industry. Eventually, there may likely come a time when there will be too many Native American casinos or the growth of non-Native American casinos will create strong competition. When and if this comes, Native American casinos will have to move from effective developers of gambling casinos to effective marketers of gambling casi-

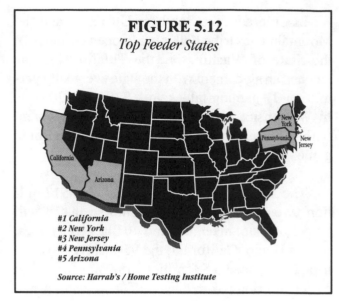

FIGURE 5.12
Top Feeder States

#1 California
#2 New York
#3 New Jersey
#4 Pennsylvania
#5 Arizona

Source: Harrah's / Home Testing Institute

nos in order to survive. Many tribal leaders, in fact, have already approached established gambling companies to seek help to better market their product.

Native-American tribes are now getting a "piece of the action" of which they have so often been left out. The gambling has provided employment for Native Americans and for other people living near the casinos, revenues for investment for the future, and monies for investment in edu-

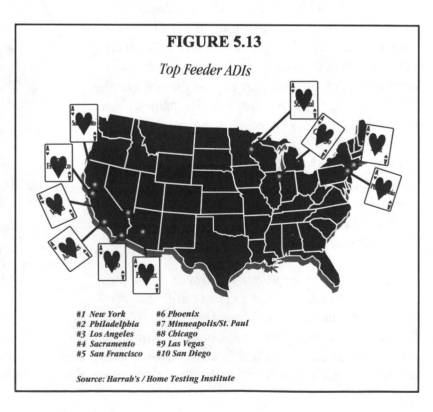

FIGURE 5.13
Top Feeder ADIs

#1 New York	#6 Phoenix
#2 Philadelphia	#7 Minneapolis/St. Paul
#3 Los Angeles	#8 Chicago
#4 Sacramento	#9 Las Vegas
#5 San Francisco	#10 San Diego

Source: Harrah's / Home Testing Institute

cation, housing, health care, and other needs on the reservation.

GENERALLY A
POPULAR ALTERNATIVE

In only a few short years, casino gambling has spread from only two states to the point where it has been approved, in some form, in a total of 21 states. (This does not include gambling on Indian reservations which is discussed in Chapter III.) With the adoption of lotteries by the vast majority of states, the inhibitions often tied with gambling have been dropping — after all, if the state government urges that a person gamble, how bad can it be?

In addition, increasing financial demands on state and local governments, coupled with a strong voter resistance to increased taxes, and in many cases, a declining economy, have forced them to look for other alternatives to raising money. Like lotteries, casino gambling has been seen as a painless way of raising money, a "fun" or a "voluntary" form of taxation.

But Some Have Turned It Down

That does not mean that every state or locality has supported casino gambling. Floridians have periodically voted casino gambling down, but it likely will return to the ballot. Casino supporters in Arizona could not raise enough signatures to get the issue of casino gambling on the ballot. Alaskans rejected casino gambling by a margin of almost 2 to 1, while Ohio voters also refused casino gambling by a similar proportion. Chicago decided against casino gambling, although riverboats from neighboring Indiana may fulfill some Chicagoans need to gamble.

Nonetheless, for many states and localities, casino gambling is considered a way to reverse economic decline and raise revenue. From an economic standpoint, the expansion of the opportunity to introduce casino gambling is seen as a growing business opportunity. Gambling businesses

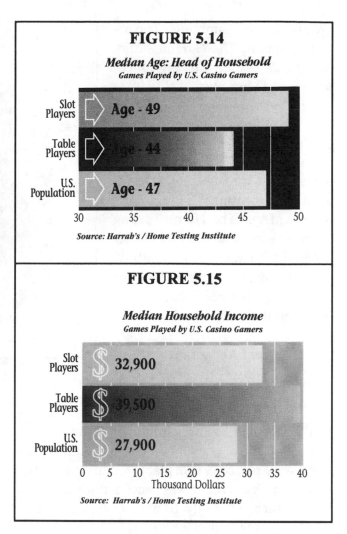

FIGURE 5.14

Median Age: Head of Household
Games Played by U.S. Casino Gamers

Slot Players — Age - 49
Table Players — Age - 44
U.S. Population — Age - 47

Source: Harrah's / Home Testing Institute

FIGURE 5.15

Median Household Income
Games Played by U.S. Casino Gamers

Slot Players — $32,900
Table Players — $39,500
U.S. Population — $27,900

Thousand Dollars

Source: Harrah's / Home Testing Institute

believe there is a large, unmet demand for casino gambling throughout the United States. The successes of gambling in South Dakota and Colorado, of riverboat gambling on the Mississippi and other waterways, at Ledyard in Connecticut, and the casinos on Native American reservations in Minnesota, Wisconsin, and other states, and the increases in casino gambling on cruise ships would seem to indicate they are right. Like any other business, gambling will continue to grow until the needs of the consumer are met. It is likely to be some time before that need is filled.

THE HARRAH'S SURVEY OF CASINO
GAMING ENTERTAINMENT

Harrah's Casino Hotels is one of the major operators of gambling casinos in the United States. In 1991, Harrah's hired the Home Testing Institute (New York City) to survey gamblers' attitudes

61

towards casino gambling. The resulting report, *The Harrah's Survey of U.S. Casino Gaming Entertainment* (Memphis, TN, 1993) also includes findings from surveys by the *Yenkelovich Clancy Shulman Monitor*, an annual national survey of attitudes and values and the Communication Development Company (West Des Moines, IA). The Home Testing Institute surveyed 100,000 households from which they identified 15,800 gamblers. The majority of findings in *Harrah's Survey* are based on their responses.

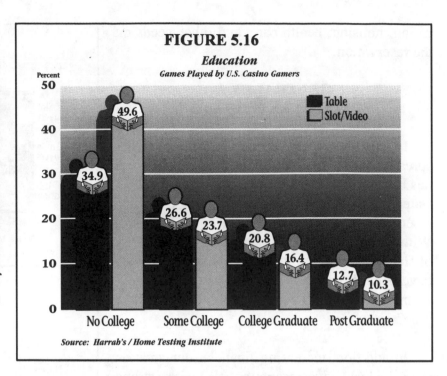

FIGURE 5.16
Education
Games Played by U.S. Casino Gamers

Source: *Harrah's / Home Testing Institute*

General Acceptance of Casino Gambling

The *Harrah Survey* found that the public generally accepted casino gambling. About 55 percent of all those questioned thought casino gambling was "perfectly acceptable for anyone," while 35 percent believed it was "acceptable for others, but not for me." Only 10 percent thought casino gambling was "not acceptable for anyone." (See Figure 5.7.)

Harrah's Survey indicated that about 50 percent of the U.S. adult population had gambled at a casino at some time during their life, up 50 percent from 33 percent only four years before in 1989 (Figure 5.8). Almost 22 percent of U.S. households had gone to a casino to gamble in 1991, up from 18 percent in 1990 (Figure 5.9). *The Harrah's Survey* found the typical casino gambler earning more (Figure 5.10) and was somewhat better educated (Figure 5.11) than the general U.S. population.

Where Do the Casino Players Come From?

Most gamblers came from the West and Northeast. Not surprisingly, the top five feeder states (California, New York, New Jersey, Pennsylvania, and Arizona), which accounted for 46 percent of all casino gamblers and 56 percent of all casino

TABLE 5.11
Customer Traits By Casino Gaming Destination

All gaming markets have some unique differences in terms of customer characteristics.

LAS VEGAS — Only true national draw, higher mix from North Central and West.

LAUGHLIN — Older, empty-nester couples, largely from the West.

LAKE TAHOE — Younger, well-educated, slightly more singles; more ethnic diversity and predominantly from Western states.

RENO — Some ethnic diversity and predominantly from Western states.

ATLANTIC CITY — Older, more singles, primarily from the Northeast.

RIVERBOATS — Older, more likely married, and living in North Central states; demographics very similar to Atlantic City.

INDIAN GAMING — Less likely to have attended college, from North Central region.

CRUISE SHIP — More affluent, well educated, fewer children, largely from the South.

FOREIGN CASINOS — Highly affluent, much younger, very well-educated, more likely single, higher ethnic diversity, Northeast and Southern states.

Source: *Harrah's / Home Testing Institute*

trips, were located near Nevada and Atlantic City. (See Figure 5.12.) Similarly, the top 10 ADIs (Areas of Dominant Influence, or TV markets around major metropolitan areas), which accounted for 45 percent of all gamblers and 58 percent of all gambling trips in 1991, were generally also near Nevada and Atlantic City. (See Figure 5.13.) The position of Minneapolis-Saint Paul at number seven is a result of the rapid expansion of gambling on Native American reservations in that state.

What Did Casino Gamblers Play?

Sixty-eight percent of all casino gamblers played the slot/video games, while 32 percent gambled on the table games most frequently. The typical slot machine player (49 years) was older than the typical table player (44 years) (Figure 5.14), while the typical table player earned more ($39,500) than the typical slot machine gambler ($32,900)(Figure 5.15). Table players tended to be more educated than slot machine players. (See Figure 5.16.) Table 5.11 shows the different characteristics among the customers at the various gambling places.

CASINOS AROUND THE WORLD

Casino gambling is very common around the world. The casinos in Monte Carlo are probably the most famous. Although there are four casinos in Monte Carlo, the elegant Casino of Monte Carlo is probably the most well-known. There are 12 state-operated casinos in Austria and eight in Belgium. France has more than 100 casinos, many of them as beautiful as the Casino of Monte Carlo and many are located in such exotic places as Biarritz and Cannes.

Almost all of Germany's 25 casinos are located in spas, probably the most famous of which is the luxurious casino at Baden-Baden. The more than 100 casinos in the United Kingdom are called "private clubs." Portugal has six casinos and Spain has almost 40 casinos.

While the residents of Hong Kong cannot legally gamble, they can take a 75 minute hydrofoil ride to the nearby Portuguese colony of Macao where they can choose from eight casinos. They could also fly to Australia and try their luck in the casinos down under.

In the Caribbean, people may gamble at the hotel casinos of Puerto Rico or Aruba. Almost all the tourists who fly to the Bahamas visit the country's four casinos. There are relatively few casinos in Latin America and South America, although Argentina has ten. Otherwise, most other Latin American and South American countries have just one or two casinos.

In October 1993, Canada opened its first casino in Montreal, Quebec at the site of the 1967 World Exposition French Pavilion and another casino in the Charlevoix region of Quebec is being considered. In the Province of Ontario, the government has awarded a preliminary agreement to the partnership of Ceasers World, Inc, Circus Enterprises, Ltd., and Hilton Hotels to build a $300 million gambling and entertainment complex in Windsor, Ontario, directly across the river from Detroit, Michigan. The casino is expected to open in the summer of 1996.

CHAPTER VI

BINGO AND OTHER CHARITABLE GAMES

HOW MUCH MONEY IS BET ON CHARITY GAMING

The National Association of Fundraising Ticket Manufacturers (NAFTM) periodically surveys states permitting charitable activities to determine how much money is raised at charity gaming throughout the United States. Charity gaming activities include bingo, charity game tickets, pull-tabs, jar tickets, breakopens, instant bingo, Lucky 7's, pickle cards, raffles, casino nights, and various other games of chance. Their survey does not include statistics for gaming conducted on Native American reservations. (For information on gambling on Native-American reservations, see Chapter III.) Statistics are based on completed responses from 32 states and 7 Canadian provinces.

The NAFTM estimates* that over $6.4 billion was wagered in 1992 in charity gaming in the United States. Minnesota ($1.26 billion) was, by far, the number one charity game state, followed by Washington State ($704 million) and Texas ($665 million). Approximately $1.9 billion was bet in Canada, most of it in Alberta ($698 million) and

---

* The NAFTM estimate of total handle, the amount of money wagered, is based on the information provided by only the states that responded to their survey. Eugene Martin Christiensen, in *Gaming and Wagering Business,* estimates total handle for the whole country. Therefore, Christiensen's estimates will be higher than those of the NAFTM.

TABLE 6.1
GROSS RECEIPTS BREAKDOWN

State	Annual Gross Receipts
AK	$ 214,077,273
AZ	50,300,430
CO	224,194,075
CT	59,966,000
DC	5,317,682
FL	42,590,136
GA	37,208,691
IL	260,043,907
IN	149,645,176
IA	59,330,037
KS	30,776,111
LA	398,551,587
MA	267,800,000
MI	302,628,256
MN	1,262,569,000
MS[1]	45,712,964
MO	190,048,219
NE[2]	201,984,634
NH	83,963,398
NM	77,893,426
NC	39,154,128
ND	273,055,070
OH	653,172,500
OR	63,562,748
TX	665,250,592
WA[2]	703,551,637
WI	59,746,546
TOTAL:	**$6,422,094,223**

Province	Annual Gross Receipts
ALB	$ 697,921,664
BC	609,700,000
NEWB	69,500,599
NEWF	90,214,202
NOVA	105,100,000
PEI	17,401,152
SASK	312,729,762
TOTAL:	**$1,902,567,379**

Total U.S. & Canada: **$8,324,661,602**

[1] Reported for a six-month period
[2] Some commercial activity included

Source: *1992 Report on Charity Gaming in North America,* National Association of Fundraising Ticket Manufacturers, (Bismarck, ND, 1993)

British Columbia ($610 million).* (See Table 6.1.) Charity gaming tickets (46 percent) and bingo (42 percent) account for almost the total handle (Figure 6.1).

BINGO — FROM UNKNOWN ORIGINS TO A UNIQUELY AMERICAN GAME

Historians are unsure of the origin of bingo. Experts attribute it to the English, the Dutch, or the Swedes. Others believe bingo developed either from the 16th century Italian game of lotto, or from the popular lottery game of keno, first played in New Orleans during the 1840s. In the 1920s, bingo was played at local movie theaters. Operated as a "raffle" to avoid state laws against certain forms of gambling, the movie theater games were the first to make bingo a form of public entertainment. The winner of the "raffle" drawing would shout "Bingo!" and claim the prize.

Modern-day bingo, also known as beano, is a simple game. It is based entirely on chance and played until a participant wins. Players purchase a bingo card which is made of cardboard or paper and contains five rows of five squares each. (At the end of the session, the cards are returned to the game manager to be used again.) One letter of the word BINGO appears above each of the vertical columns. All of the squares contain a number from 1 to 75, except the "free" center square.

In a typical game, an announcer calls a letter/number combination, such as "B-15." As a combination is called, players who have that combination on their card place a "bean" or cardboard circle on the correct square. When a player has covered five squares in a vertical, horizontal, or diagonal column, he or she shouts "Bingo." The announcer then checks the player's card against a master card, and, if the cards match, the player receives a prize and a new game begins.

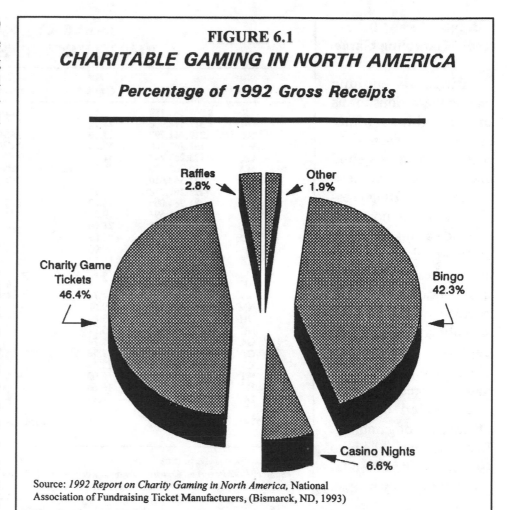

FIGURE 6.1
CHARITABLE GAMING IN NORTH AMERICA
Percentage of 1992 Gross Receipts

Raffles 2.8%
Other 1.9%
Charity Game Tickets 46.4%
Bingo 42.3%
Casino Nights 6.6%

Source: *1992 Report on Charity Gaming in North America,* National Association of Fundraising Ticket Manufacturers, (Bismarck, ND, 1993)

---

* Games of chance may be regulated at the state or local level, fiscal years may vary from state to state, and different agencies provide different types and amounts of information. In addition, some charitable gambling is not reported. Therefore, NAFTM advises that figures in its reports should be considered estimates.

Bingo — The "Innocent" Gambling Game

Bingo is unique among the various forms of gambling. Many Americans learned to play the game as a child and do not consider it to be gambling. Bingo sessions are a common form of fund-raising by charitable organizations such as churches, synagogues, or service clubs, so many people view the game as socially and morally acceptable. This gives bingo a respectability that, until recently, was not enjoyed by most other forms of gambling. Even commercial bingo (see below) is viewed favorably by many people.

	TABLE 6.2				
	BINGO RECEIPTS				
State	*Gross Receipts*	*Per Capita**		*Province*	*Gross Receipts*
TX	$ 501,365,169	29.51		ALB	$ 329,295,853
OH	311,514,900	28.72		BC	220,300,000
MI	219,961,797	23.66		SASK	134,661,356
WA	191,767,600	39.24		NOVA	90,000,000
LA	173,203,247	41.04		NEWB	62,917,072
MA	160,700,000	26.71		NEWF	40,390,405
IL	157,362,060	13.77		PEI	11,901,152
MO	121,267,778	23.70			
MN	81,784,000	18.69		TOTAL:	$889,465,838
CO	63,656,594	19.33			
OR	61,573,303	21.66			
ND	58,168,304	91.03			
IA	52,851,872	19.03			
AZ	50,300,430	13.72			
IN	49,081,928	8.85			
AK	48,112,014	87.48		*Total U.S.*	
MS[1]	45,712,964	17.77		*& Canada:*	$3,520,097,558
NM	43,944,268	29.01			
NH	39,755,233	35.85			
NC	39,154,128	5.91			
GA	37,208,691	5.74			
CT	31,500,000	9.58			
KS	30,776,111	12.42			
WI	29,750,969	6.09			
NE	26,292,995	16.66			
DC[1]	3,865,365	6.37			
TOTAL:	$2,630,631,720			* *Based on 1990 Census Bureau statistics*	

[1] Includes gross receipts for CGTs

Source: *1992 Report on Charity Gaming in North America,* National Association of Fundraising Ticket Manufacturers, (Bismarck, ND, 1993)

Charitable Bingo Games Run by Commercial Bingo Operations

In most states, bingo games are legal only when they are operated as "charitable gaming activities," that is, at least part of the handle must go to a charitable (or non-profit religious, educational, etc.) organization. Some charitable organizations run their own bingo games, but many have turned to commercial operators to run the games for them. These commercial operators may set up permanent bingo parlors where players can find a game going at almost any time of the day or night.

For their services, commercial bingo operators charge a commission on the proceeds of every game. Their commission is deducted from the "do-

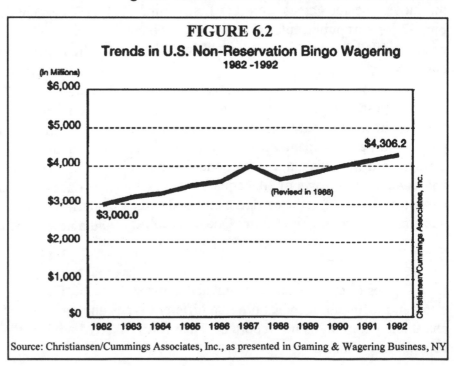

FIGURE 6.2

Trends in U.S. Non-Reservation Bingo Wagering
1982 -1992

(In Millions)

$4,306.2

(Revised in 1988)

$3,000.0

Christiansen/Cummings Associates, Inc.

Source: Christiansen/Cummings Associates, Inc., as presented in Gaming & Wagering Business, NY

nations" to the charitable organization, thereby reducing the charitable organization's revenue. But because professional operators have the time and money to invest in large-scale operations, charitable organizations generally realize more revenue than if they tried to operate the games themselves.

Almost Anyone Can Play

Only Arkansas, Hawaii, Tennessee, and Utah do not permit bingo. The National Association of Fundraising Ticket Manufacturers (NAFTM) estimated the gross handle for bingo in 1992 at about $2.6 billion in the United States and $889.5 million in Canada. *Gaming and Wagering Business* estimated bingo wagering in the United States at $4.3 billion in 1992, considerably higher than the NAFTM estimate.

According to the NAFTM, Texas ($501 million), Ohio ($312 million), and Michigan ($220 million) had the greatest handle in the United States, while Alberta ($329 million) and British Columbia ($220 million) had the largest handles in Canada. (See Table 6.2.) Prize payouts averaged 75 percent in 1992, ranging from 85 percent in Alaska to 58 percent in Georgia. Similarly, *Gaming and Wagering Business* estimated the amount of the handle retained was 25 percent, meaning that about 75 percent was paid out in prizes.

Eugene Martin Christiensen, writing in *Gaming and Wagering Business* believes that bingo is a mature sector of the gambling industry. This means that the public's demand for bingo has been met and, as a result, revenues from bingo have levelled off and are unlikely to grow in the future. (See Figure 6.2.) Christiensen also thinks the spread of casino gambling may likely hurt bingo's future as bingo players find another way to spend their money.

TABLE 6.3
CHARITY GAME TICKETS

State	Gross Receipts	Per Capita*	% Payout	# Games Sold
MN	$1,157,419,000	$264.55	81%	584,887
WA[1]	490,806,600	100.43	67%	1,534,606
OH[2]	341,657,600	31.50	75%	N/A
LA	214,892,099	50.92	79%	102,690
NE	172,590,076	109.37	74%	92,403
ND	164,506,669	257.44	80%	135,000[2]
TX	163,885,423	9.65	67%	N/A
AK	157,504,510	286.37	77%	N/A
CO	155,025,236	47.06	N/A	N/A
IL	90,635,880	7.93	N/A	N/A
IN	87,881,096	15.85	N/A	N/A
MA	82,700,000	13.75	60%	102,690
MO	68,780,441	13.44	N/A	N/A
NH	44,208,165	39.86	72%	71,552
MI	36,944,265	3.97	73%	25,845
NM	33,009,720	21.79	74%	N/A
CT	12,570,000	3.82	64%	7,874
TOTAL:	$3,475,016,780			

* Based on 1990 Census Bureau statistics

Province	Gross Receipts	% Payout
SASK	$124,383,195	74%
BC[3]	119,700,000	65%
ALB	98,977,934	74%
NEWF	42,172,393	73%
NOVA	5,000,000	80%
NEWB	779,643	66%
TOTAL:	$391,013,165	

Total U.S. & Canada: $3,866,029,945

[1] Includes commercial activity; approximately $113,957,492 is non-profit amount
[2] Estimate by state official
[3] Includes commercial activity

Source: *1992 Report on Charity Gaming in North America*, National Association of Fundraising Ticket Manufacturers, (Bismarck, ND, 1993)

67

Bingo on Native American Reservations

These figures do not, however, include bingo on Native American reservations, however, which has grown dramatically and has been cutting into non-reservation bingo games. The handle on bingo played on Native American has risen from almost nothing a decade ago to $1.4 billion in 1992. Meanwhile, revenues earned from bingo reached $429 million in 1992.

Nonetheless, bingo on Native American reservations has also levelled off with the handle up only 2 percent from 1991 to 1992. Just as non-reservation bingo has been affected by the expansion of casino gambling, so has Native American bingo. The returns will continue to be affected as more Native American tribes continue to open up casinos next door to existing bingo halls. Of course, in many of these cases, the money will go into the same tribal coffers no matter which form of gambling they choose.

Regulation and Enforcement

Despite bingo's popularity as a charity fund-raiser and its reputation as a harmless pastime, it is as susceptible to abuses as any other form of gambling. Racketeers are suspected of

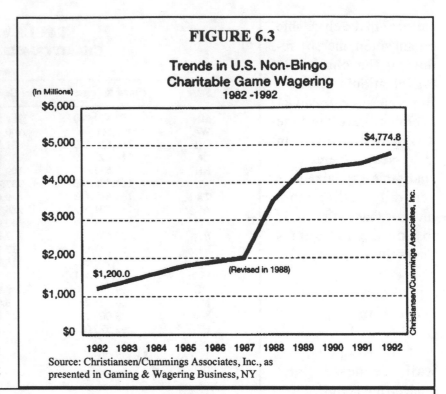

FIGURE 6.3

Trends in U.S. Non-Bingo Charitable Game Wagering
1982-1992

Source: Christiansen/Cummings Associates, Inc., as presented in Gaming & Wagering Business, NY

TABLE 6.4
RAFFLE RECEIPTS

State	Annual Gross Receipts	Province	Annual Gross Receipts
MI	$ 30,006,534	BC	$ 31,200,000
WI	29,995,577	ALB	26,360,905
MA	19,500,000	SASK	16,532,313
CT	14,300,000	NOVA	10,000,000
AK	6,454,552	NEWF	6,344,756
CO	5,512,245	NEWB	5,318,618
LA[1]	5,059,646	PEI	5,000,000
IA	5,052,968		
IN	4,938,599	TOTAL:	$100,756,592
WA	3,532,058		
MN	3,267,000		
NE[2]	3,101,563		
OR	1,989,445		
ND	1,238,955		
DC	1,071,640		
NM	939,438		
TOTAL:	$135,960,230		

Total U.S. & Canada: $236,716,822

[1] Includes casino night receipts

[2] Includes some non-profit lotteries

Source: *1992 Report on Charity Gaming in North America,* National Association of Fundraising Ticket Manufacturers, (Bismarck, ND, 1993)

controlling some commercial bingo operations; however, when commercial bingo games are held under the sponsorship of a charitable organization, questions are seldom asked. Skimming — the practice of under-reporting income from games and pocketing the difference — is thought to be the biggest problem facing officials who enforce bingo regulations. As with other forms of gambling, it is required that the revenues from bingo operations be reported to the government. The government considers skimmed money as not just stolen money, but also as untaxed money. Therefore, both charitable groups and the government, through the loss of tax revenue, lose money when it is skimmed off by dishonest bingo operators.

Almost all states require bingo licenses, but few have license control boards. Law enforcement officials generally ignore illegal or dishonest bingo games because their efforts to regulate them are resisted by the general public. Few municipal or state budgets have funds for bingo investigation. In addition, many police officers believe bingo is a "victimless" crime, too insignificant to merit substantial enforcement time and effort. As a result, bingo continues to be a form of gambling that has the potential for large revenues with little regulation by government or law enforcement agencies.

CHARITY GAMES

In 1992, charity games were permitted for use by non-profit organizations in 33 states and 6 provinces. According to the NAFTM, far more money was wagered on charitable games in the United States than bingo ($3.5 billion compared to $2.6 billion), while about $391 million was bet on charity games in Canada. Minnesota ($1.2 billion) had, by far, the greatest amount of money wagered on charity games, followed by Washington ($491 million) and Ohio ($342 million). In Canada, Saskatchewan ($124 million), British Columbia ($120 million) and Alberta ($99 million) had the largest handles. (See Table 6.3.) Typical payouts were around 72 percent, ranging from 81 percent in Minnesota to 60 percent in Massachusetts.

TABLE 6.5
CASINO NIGHTS

State	Gross Receipts
MI	$15,715,660
IL	12,045,967
MA	4,900,000
IN	951,634
WA	944,443
IA	612,834
DC	380,677
CT	346,000
AK	315,417
TOTAL:	$36,212,632

Province	Gross Receipts
ALB	$243,286,972
BC	238,500,000
SASK	37,152,898
PEI	500,000
NOVA	100,000
NEWF	86,000
NEWB	77,289
TOTAL:	$519,703,159

Total U.S. & Canada: $555,915,791

Source: *1992 Report on Charity Gaming in North America*, National Association of Fundraising Ticket Manufacturers, (Bismarck, ND, 1993)

Eugene Christiensen, in *Gaming and Wagering Business*, estimated that about $4.8 billion was wagered on non-bingo charitable games, producing about $1.3 billion in revenues for a retained amount of 27 percent, or a payout of around 73 percent. Unlike bingo wagering, which has been levelling off, the betting on non-bingo charitable gaming has been growing. (See Figure 6.3.) Nonetheless, Christiensen still wonders how well charitable gambling will withstand the spread of casino gambling.

RAFFLES

Many states that permit raffles do not require organizations that operate them to report them to the state. As a result, the NAFTM notes that the gross proceeds figure is only a fraction of the ac-

TABLE 6.6

TAX AND LICENSE FEE REVENUE

State	Tax Revenue Generated	License Fees Generated	Total Fees	Use of Revenue
AK	$ 1,270,000[1]	$ 330,000	$ 1,600,000	N/A
AZ	876,586	25,300	901,886	General fund
CO	1,016,113	162,063	1,178,176	Administer and enforce bingo/raffles law
CT	1,726,000	93,185	1,819,185	General fund
DC	N/A	6,170	6,170	General fund
FL	2,975,641	159,120	3,134,761	Collected by state government
GA	1,488,348	27,400	1,515,748	General fund
IL	12,761,276	1,105,666	13,866,942	License fee: administrative support and allocation to local governments for enforcement
IN	484,765	1,256,755	1,741,520	Charity gaming enforcement fund; surplus to Build Indiana Fund; credit to state and local capital projects account
IA	2,669,850	180,000	2,849,850	General fund
KS	926,354	17,325	943,679	Tax: 1/3 general fund, 1/3 enforcement by DOR, 1/3 to cities and counties; License fee: general fund
LA	1,591,171	486,190	2,077,361	Dedicated by statute for regulation of industry
MA	17,520,000	37,950	17,557,950	Beano: 3/5 general fund, 2/5 lottery for administration; Raffles/Casino: general fund; CGTs: 50% purchase and selling, 50% local aid; Bingo license fees: to lottery subject to appropriation
MI	4,697,367[1]	847,925	5,545,292	License fee: administration expenses
MN	56,903,000	1,465,000	58,368,000	General fund
MS	345,325	326,423	671,748	Enforcement
MO	4,751,205	691,000	5,442,205	General revenue fund

[1] CGTs only

TAX AND LICENSE FEE REVENUE CONTINUED

State	Tax Revenue Generated	License Fees Generated	Total Fees	Use of Revenue
NE	6,084,856	368,698	6,453,554	General fund and enforcement
NH	1,808,606	433,537	2,242,143	Aid to education
NM	355,994	30,000	385,994	General fund
NC	N/A	37,600	37,600	General fund
ND	9,537,337	196,000	9,733,337	General fund except $680,000 paid to cities and counties for gaming enforcement and $100,000 paid to AG's office for gaming enforcement
OH	N/A	130,000	130,000	N/A
OR	601,267	41,480	642,747	Regulate charitable gaming
SC	7,214,275[2]		7,214,275	50% general fund; 37½% Parks, Recs and Tourism; 12½% Aging Commission
SD	37,497	60,000	97,497	General fund
TX	28,416,300	3,765,025	32,181,325	General fund
WA[3]	24,475,297	6,147,914	30,623,211	Tax: local level used primarily to enforce laws and rules; License fee: regulation
WI	595,019	383,148	978,167	Tax: general fund; License fee: offset operating costs, balance to general fund

Province	Tax Revenue Generated	License Fees Generated	Total Fees	Use of Revenue
ALB	$ N/A	$ 4,045,999	$ 4,045,999	Gaming administration and enforcement
BC	11,070,000	38,900,000	49,970,000	General revenue fund
NEWB	N/A	13,990	13,990	N/A
NEWF	N/A	694,031	694,031	Administering Lotteries Control Program (amounts change due to issuance of refunds)
NOVA	1,371,000[2]		1,371,000	Tax: general fund; License fee: Licensees' projects and programs
PEI	N/A	209,557	209,557	General revenue fund
SASK	6,681,359[2]		6,681,359	Education, culture, recreation, religious, relief of poverty, community benefit

[2] Includes license fees
[3] Includes some revenue from commercial activity

Source: *1992 Report on Charity Gaming in North America*, National Association of Fundraising Ticket Manufacturers, (Bismarck, ND, 1993)

tual amount bet. Sixteen states reported raffle wagering of about $136 million, while seven Canadian provinces reported $100.8 million. (See Table 6.4.)

CASINO NIGHTS

Casino nights, also called Las Vegas nights, Monte Carlo, and Millionaire Parties, are another popular form of charitable fund raising. In most states, players are charged admission at the door and they receive "play money" which they then can bet on various games. Nine states reported casino night wagering of $36.2 million in 1990. Casino nights were far more popular in Canada with seven provinces reporting wagering of $519.7 million. (See Table 6.5.) Undoubtedly the future of casino nights is at risk when players will likely be offered the opportunity to play in real casinos with the opportunity to win real winnings.

HOW MUCH WENT TO TAX REVENUE?

According to the NAFTM, charitable gaming in 29 states through taxes and license fees contributed about $209.9 million in 1992 to the various states. State and local treasuries in Minnesota ($58.4 million), Texas ($32.2 million) and Washington ($30.6 million) benefitted the most. Seven Canadian provinces took in about $63 million. (See Table 6.6.)

AND HOW MUCH WENT TO CHARITY?

The NAFTM reported that in the 23 states that reported net proceeds, $721.8 million was raised

TABLE 6.7
THE BOTTOM LINE

State	Net Proceeds	% Gross Receipts	Per Capita*
AK	$ 17,522,098	8.18%	31.86
AZ	10,255,327	20.39%	2.80
CO	33,870,397	15.11%	10.28
CT	20,127,500	33.56%	6.12
DC	1,688,053	31.74%	2.78
FL	2,975,641	6.99%	.23
GA	13,755,725	36.97%	2.12
IN	30,217,229	20.19%	5.45
IA	10,700,658	18.03%	3.85
LA	49,077,160	12.31%	11.63
MA	53,670,000	20.04%	8.92
MI	69,006,158	22.80%	7.42
MN	78,614,000	6.23%	17.97
NE	25,292,722	12.52%	16.03
NH	10,875,478	12.95%	9.81
NM	11,846,067	15.21%	7.82
NC	3,053,849	7.80%	.46
ND	21,018,309	7.70%	32.89
OH	80,576,500	12.34%	7.43
OR	8,555,450	13.46%	3.01
TX	67,156,230	10.09%	3.95
WA[1]	84,443,277	12.00%	17.28
WI[2]	17,532,217	58.45%	3.58

TOTAL: $721,830,045   * Based on 1990 Census Bureau statistics

Province	Net Proceeds	% Gross Receipts
ALB	$101,848,271	14.59%
BC	115,300,000	18.91%
NB	15,778,228	22.70%
NEWF	15,976,945	17.71%
NOVA	34,979,000	33.28%
PEI[3]	1,740,625	14.63%
SASK	51,606,771	16.50%

TOTAL: $337,229,840

Total U.S. & Canada: $1,059,059,885

[1]Includes some commercial activity
[2]Raffles only
[3]Bingo only

Source: *1992 Report on Charity Gaming in North America,* National Association of Fundraising Ticket Manufacturers, (Bismarck, ND, 1993)

for charitable organizations in 1992, about 12 percent of the gross handle. In Canada, about $337.2 million was raised for charity, about 18 percent of the reported gross handle. (See Table 6.7.)

CHAPTER VII

LOTTERIES — LEGAL AND ALLURING

DEFINITION

A lottery is a game in which people purchase numbered tickets in the hope of winning a prize if the number on their ticket is the one drawn from a pool of all the tickets purchased for that particular event. In the case of instant lotteries, the bettor wins if the ticket contains a pre-determined winning number. Raffles are a form of lottery in which the prize is usually goods rather than cash. Raffles are most often conducted by churches or charitable organizations and are relatively small in size. As of December 1993, lotteries were legal in 37 states, Washington, DC, the Virgin Islands, and Puerto Rico.

A PART OF OUR HERITAGE

Lotteries have been a part of American life since the settlement of Jamestown by the Virginia Company of London. Prior to the establishment of a regular tax system, lotteries were the most effective means of raising money to finance public works, churches, schools, and universities. Even after the American Revolution, lotteries remained the most popular form of fund-raising for public services. Some of the nation's most prestigious banks, including the Chase Manhattan Bank and First City National Bank of New York, were founded by former lottery managers.

Although lotteries appeared to be an easy way to raise money, the discovery during the 1830s of corruption and fraud among some lottery managers and public officials resulted in a flurry of reform laws. Continued opposition to lotteries was voiced by a small number of newspapers through their editorials and by the Society of Friends (Quakers). Other religious groups did not object to lotteries because they used them to finance new church construction. Most newspapers did not object to lotteries because lottery operators were big newspaper advertisers.

Eventually, however, many newspapers did join the anti-lottery crusade. By 1840, lotteries were abolished in most northern states. During the next 20 years, the number of lottery operations in the South and West also decreased, but some were revived after the Civil War to finance reconstruction efforts. Corruption and fraud continued to be a problem, however, forcing the federal government to enact a number of anti-lottery bills between 1860 and 1895 which ultimately banished lotteries (except for the Louisiana Lottery, see Chapter I) for the next 40 years.

THE MODERN LOTTERY

During the Depression Era of the 1930s, the United States was flooded with lottery tickets from the Caribbean, Latin America, and the Irish Sweepstakes, reviving interest in lottery gambling. Following hearings on organized crime before the Special Senate Committee to Investigate Organized Crime in Interstate Commerce (Kefauver Hearings, 1950), Congress approved the Revenue Act of 1951, which called for the purchase of a $50 occupational tax stamp and a 10 percent excise tax on gross receipts from wagering businesses. Although designed to tax and control other forms of gambling, the Revenue Act opened the door for the establishment of legal lottery games.*

In 1964, New Hampshire became the first state in the 20th century to legalize lottery games. Funds raised were to be used for educational programs in local municipalities. New York followed with a state lottery in 1967, but the real revitalization of lottery games occurred in 1971 when New Jersey introduced a computer-based, 50-cent weekly game and increased the size of the prize pool to 45 percent of the gross amount wagered. The New Jersey system was later adopted by New Hampshire and New York.

In 1974, the federal Commission on the Review of the National Policy Toward Gambling (referred to hereafter as the National Gambling Commission) held hearings to investigate the 19th century anti-lottery statutes. State lottery directors claimed that these statutes did not allow states to develop their own policies on gambling or to conduct business and raise revenues as they wished without undue federal regulation or interference. As a result of the Commission's findings, the 93rd Congress passed legislation allowing states to advertise on radio and television and to send lottery information and tickets through the mail within the borders of their own state.

Lotteries did not develop nationwide until the 1980s. The federal government was transferring more financial responsibilities to the states at the same time that citizens were becoming increasingly reluctant to pay more taxes. State and local governments were becoming desperate for money. Lotteries were seen as an easy way to raise large sums of revenues without upsetting most voters. The lotteries were often presented as a form of voluntary taxation and most states have directed that money gained from lotteries is to be used for purposes with which few voters could quarrel, such as education or aid to the elderly.

The nationwide adoption and promotion of lotteries by the states has contributed to a major change in attitude towards gambling throughout the United States. Gambling has generally lost the image of sin to which it had once been connected. With the strong public acceptance of lotteries, gambling is now more likely to be seen as entertainment and fun rather than a violation of generally accepted morality. The connection it once had with organized crime has long been forgotten. This change in attitude has been a major factor in the recent boom of huge casino/hotels in Las Vegas designed to attract the entire family to a complete entertainment experience of which gambling, while still the driving engine, is only a part. (See Chapter V.)

TYPES OF LOTTERY GAMES

Instant Lottery

Instant lotteries were first introduced in Massachusetts in 1974. For $1, a player buys a ticket and immediately finds out if he or she has picked a winning number. Instant tickets have a coating which the player scratches off to uncover the number or symbol underneath that reveals whether or not the ticket is a "winning ticket." Instant lotteries are commonly the first type of lottery established by previously non-lottery states. Every state that has legalized lotteries has an instant lottery.

Numbers — or Pick 3, Pick 4

In 1975, New Jersey was the first state to legalize numbers, a formerly illegal game (see Chapter VIII). In the most common form of numbers, a

---

* Few local gamblers would buy the federal occupational tax stamp because it would tell local authorities that the person was a gambler. Paying the excise tax would also expose the gambler. Since gambling was illegal in all but one state, this law virtually made gambling a federal as well as a state crime.

TABLE 7.1

U.S. lottery fiscal year sales, '92 vs. '93

(in $ millions, unaudited[1])

Lottery	Population	1992 sales	1993 sales	% change	1992 profit	1993 profit	% change	Per cap. sales
Ariz.	3.8	$249.3	$259.0	3.8%	$91.6	$93.1	1.6%	$67
Calif.	30.87	1,359.0	1,760.0	29.5%	464.9	620.0	33.4%	57
Colo.	3.47	239.2	263.5	10.1%	76.0	73.5	-3.4%	76
Conn.	3.28	543.9	552.6	1.6%	204.5	221.7	8.4%	168
D.C.[2]	0.59	147.0	180.0	22.4%	48.5	55.0	13.4%	305
Del.	0.69	78.1	90.1	15.4%	27.7	29.0	4.7%	130
Fla.	13.48	2,227.2	2,169.7	-2.6%	862.1	876.0	1.6%	161
Idaho	1.07	51.7	57.3	10.8%	12.6	14.0	11.1%	53
Ill.	11.63	1,636.9	1,575.5	-3.8%	612.2	587.4	-4.2%	135
Ind.	5.88	390.1	513.6	31.7%	116.2	146.4	25.9%	87
Iowa	2.81	165.2	207.2	25.4%	46.0	53.8	16.9%	74
Kan.	2.52	77.0	114.1	48.2%	23.8	32.6	37.0%	45
Kent.	3.75	438.6	486.5	10.9%	103.4	99.3	-4.1%	130
La.	4.29	380.2	492.7	29.6%	139.6	188.8	35.2%	115
Maine	1.23	113.5	118.0	3.9%	35.4	36.5	3.1%	96
Md.	4.78	812.3	882.2	8.6%	302.0	323.8	7.2%	184
Mass.	6.0	1,719.3	2,010.0	16.9%	520.0	550.0	5.7%	335
Mich.[3]	9.44	1,218.0	1,220.0	0.2%	477.3	N.A.	N.A.	129
Minn.	4.48	297.6	328.8	10.5%	74.0	78.5	6.1%	73
Mo.	5.19	220.4	257.0	16.6%	67.1	72.1	7.6%	50
Mont.	0.82	27.9	36.6	31.2%	5.6	8.9	59.0%	45
N.H.	1.11	111.2	112.5	1.2%	36.7	37.0	0.8%	101
N.J.	7.79	1,360.3	1,371.1	0.8%	574.2	574.2	0.0%	176
N.Y.	18.12	2,061.4	2,360.0	14.4%	666.7	1,000.0	50.0%	130
Ohio	11.02	1,685.4	1,970.0	16.9%	647.1	663.0	2.4%	179
Ore.	2.98	268.8	431.4	60.5%	72.9	137.0	87.9%	145
Pa.	12.01	1,408.9	1,427.4	1.3%	657.8	603.2	-9.1%	119
R.I.	1.005	64.6	138.0	113.6%	23.6	43.7	85.2%	137
S.D.	0.71	150.8	170.6	13.1%	43.9	55.2	25.7%	240
Texas[3]	17.66	594.0	1,714.0	N.A.	N.A.	N.A.	N.A.	97
Ver.	0.57	51.4	50.4	-1.9%	16.9	16.6	-1.8%	88
Va.	6.38	832.8	843.5	1.3%	290.8	297.1	2.2%	132
Wash.	5.14	302.2	365.0	20.8%	106.6	128.4	20.5%	71
W. Va.	1.81	90.3	115.9	28.3%	29.3	35.9	22.5%	64
Wis.	5.01	449.6	490.0	9.0%	150.2	167.0[4]	11.2%	98
Totals		$21,824[1]	$25,134[1]	15.2%[1]	$7,627[1]	$7,919[1]	3.8%[1]	

[1] Fiscal year sales are unofficial and subject to change. [2] Projected numbers. [3] Estimated numbers based on previous year's sales figures. [4] Based on net income.

Source: Eugene Martin Christiansen in *International Gaming & Wagering Business*, NY

bettor puts money on a two- or three- digit number from 00 to 999. The winning number is determined by an arbitrary mechanism, such as numbered ping-pong balls rising in an air-filled tank. State lottery administrators have found that games must be flexible in order to keep pace with the interests and demands of the public, and some states have expanded to a four-digit weekly numbers game. In 1993, 29 states, the District of Columbia, and Puerto Rico offered numbers.

Lotto

To play lotto, a bettor selects five to six numbers from a pool of 40 to 44 numbers and wagers between $1 and $4. Winning numbers are selected at random from a weekly drawing. If more than one player has the same set of numbers (in any sequence), the prize is not awarded that week and the prize money is carried forward to the next week's drawing. Lotto was first played in the

1520s in Italy using hand-painted game pieces and game boards carved from wood. In 1978, Massachusetts became the first state to offer lotto games. In 1993, 36 states, the District of Columbia, and Puerto Rico permitted lotto games.

Video Lottery

Many gaming industry observers see video lottery terminals (VLTs) as the future of the lottery industry. Until recently, video lottery was often an illegal game consisting of terminals that selected winners through computerized programs. Although still illegal in most states, many machines are operating in bars, truck stops, arcades, and convenience stores through the country.

The player inserts a quarter or a dollar bill to play a video game. This video game may be poker, keno, or dozens of other possible games. If the player wins, the machine prints out a ticket that can be cashed in at a nearby bar or grill. In many states, these video lottery games are supposed to be for entertainment only, but they are frequently used for gambling instead. This illegal payment of winnings is called the "grey market." Unlike most video games, video lottery games have little to do with skill, so that winning or losing is mainly a matter of chance. Video games are particularly attractive to young people because of their appealing graphics. Some people are concerned about the addictive nature of video lotteries. In addition, operators of other forms of gambling, most notably the regular lottery and parimutuel operations, fear, often justifiably, that VLTs will cut into their handle. For these reasons, VLTs have had a hard time getting approval in most states. VLTs have been legalized in South Dakota, West Virginia, Louisiana, Montana, Oregon, and Rhode Island.

In West Virginia and Louisiana, VLTs have been placed in racetracks in order to allay fears in the pari-mutuel industry and improve their sagging income. Rhode Island is considering putting VLTs in a greyhound track and jai-alai fronton. Racetracks are a good place to put VLTs because there

is a considerable time between races during which nothing happens as horse and dog handlers prepare for the next race. During this period many people who have come to gamble become bored. This gives them something to do while they are awaiting the next race. It also gives someone who came along to the races to be with a friend or a spouse, but who has no interest in racing, an opportunity to do something else.

LOTTERY SALES

Lotteries are big business. In 1986, lotteries surpassed casinos as the largest gambling business in America. According to Eugene Martin Christiansen in his annual survey for *Gambling and Wagering Business*, sales revenues for FY 1993 totaled $25.1 billion, up 15 percent, or $3.3 billion, from FY 1992. (See Table 7.1.) About $7.9 billion in profits went the states. Between 1982 and 1992, lottery sales increased at an average rate of 19.5 percent. Overall, *Gambling @ Wagering Business* reports that the average American in a state with a lottery wagered $103 (FY 1992), ranging from $45 in Kansas and Montana to $335 in Massachusetts and $305 in Washington, DC.

Industry observers generally believe that the lottery industry has become "mature" — that sales are levelling off because the basic demand for lotteries has been met, although the large increase from 1991 to 1992 shows that the levelling off was not quite as imminent as expected. Nonetheless, Illinois (-4 percent) and Pennsylvania (-9 percent), two of the biggest and most developed lotteries in the nation, saw declining revenues, as did Colorado (-3 percent), Kentucky (-4 percent), and Vermont (-2 percent). Arizona (2 percent), Florida (2 percent), New Hampshire (1 percent), New Jersey (0 percent), and Virginia (2 percent) had small or no increases.

Much of the growth in total lottery sales resulted from the introduction of the lottery in Texas, which immediately became a billion-dollar-lottery state, and the almost billion dollar increase in video lottery terminal sales. Therefore, while these factors and a somewhat strengthening economy made FY 1993 a strong year for lotteries, it is still likely that sales will begin to even off as soon as lottery players reach a comfortable level of betting on the lottery.

If the states expect lottery revenues to continue to grow they will have to become more innovative and come up with new games to attract new bettors and increase the wagers of those already participating. For example, Connecticut recently came out with a $25 instant win ticket for the more affluent gamblers, while at least a dozen states are introducing $2 and $5 forms of instant games, and a dozen other states are introducing various versions of Instant Monopoly to cash in on many American's fond memories of playing the game of Monopoly.

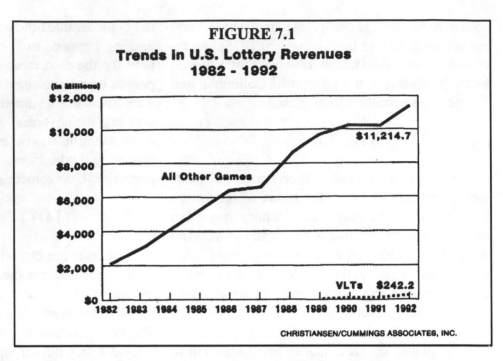

LOTTERY REVENUES

In 1992, lotteries produced $11.2 billion in revenues, up 12 percent from the year before. (See Figure 7.1.) Lotteries keep a much higher percentage of the money bet (47 percent, and 48 percent of all non-VLT bets) than any other type of gambling. (For example, the horsetrack retains 20 percent; the slot machines, 6 percent; the casinos tables, 2 percent; and bingo, 25 percent.) Therefore, while lotteries account for only 7 percent of all monies bet on gambling, they bring in 38 percent of all revenues. Overall, those who bet on the lottery won $12.9 billion.

Until recently, all state lottery revenue went into state programs. However, in 1991, New York State approved a small lottery which would benefit New York City. Proceeds from this instant lottery game would be used to help fund a crime reduction program within the City of New York.

LOTTERY AGENTS

In the United States, lottery tickets are usually sold in establishments with a lot of foot traffic, such as grocery stores, liquor stores, convenience stores, and newsstands. Establishments that sell lottery tickets must be licensed by the state and are called "agents." *Gaming and Wagering Business* reports that in FY 1992, 170,598 lottery agents earned $1.4 billion. The average commission is about 5.5 percent. The typical state pays a 5 percent commission plus various bonuses for selling winning jackpot tickets or for selling more expensive tickets. Canada's 35,050 agents earned C(anadian)$210 million (U.S.$178 million) selling tickets. In the United States, there were an average of 1,210 residents per every agent, while in Canada there were 748 residents per agent. An estimated 6 billion tickets are sold every year in North America.

In terms of the sale of instant winners, *Gaming and Wagering Business* reports that convenience stores sold 27 percent; convenience stores with gasoline, 17 percent; grocery stores, 22 percent; gas stations, 5 percent; bar/restaurants, 7 percent; drug stores, 3 percent; liquor stores, 13 percent; newstands and smoke shops, 3 percent; and others, 5 percent. The breakdown on on-line sales (sales in which the seller is directly connected by computer to a central headquarters), which includes most of the big jackpots was convenience stores, 23 percent; convenience stores with gasoline, 14 percent; grocery stores, 21 percent; gas stations, 2 percent; bar/restaurants, 3 percent; drug stores (5 percent); liquor stores, 16 percent; newstands and smoke shops, 4 percent; and others, 12 percent.

THE PLAYERS

Gaming and Wagering Business magazine surveyed lottery directors in 1985 to determine a profile of lottery players. In New Jersey, they found that about 38 percent of the players with incomes below $15,000 claimed they had no interest or very little interest in lottery games. Most persons in this category said they could not afford to play and therefore did not (although this does not explain why they were playing at the time they were surveyed). As a group, poor people played lottery games less frequently than middle- and high-income groups. Middle-income persons who had discretionary (spare) money generally considered betting on lotteries harmless fun that offered them a chance for luck to change their lives.

In 1986, several lottery market research groups developed a profile of the "typical" lottery player in Colorado and Washington. They found the average player usually played the game with the hope of winning money. Males and females in both states were equally interested in playing, but there were differences between the states in terms of age and income levels. In Colorado, most players were between 18 and 54 years and earned an average of $15,000 to $20,000 yearly. In Washington, the average player was 42 years old, with an annual income of $28,900. In both states, about 63 percent of the players had some college background or technical school experience beyond high school. Most players believed the lottery was a good way to raise money for state expenses.

In a Maine study, lottery directors found that different game formats appealed to different groups of people. One game, imaginatively named Tri-State Megabucks, was played to fulfill a fantasy, but Instant Games were played in the hope of winning money. Pick 3 and Pick 4, which are daily numbers games, were played by people who thought they had a lucky number. The state of Maine developed advertising campaigns to promote specific lottery games based on the information obtained in these marketing studies.

Dr. H. Roy Kaplan, in *Lottery Winners* (Harper and Row: New York, 1978), documented the affects of winning a lottery on the work habits of the winners. In an earlier study, conducted in 1970, Dr. Kaplan found that most people who won large sums of money quit their jobs. However, in the 1978 study, he found that the winner's degree of commitment to his or her job was related to the type of job, length of employment, educational level and income level. People who were satisfied with what they were doing tended to continue working regardless of how much money they had won. People who were unhappy at work often decided to quit their jobs, but many found different kinds of occupations at a later time.

In 1991, National Analysts interviewed 1,021 Minnesotans for Carmichael Lynch, the advertising agency for the Minnesota Lottery. They found that younger people were most likely to play the lottery with about 71 percent of those ages 18-34 having played the lottery compared to 60 percent of those age 35-64 and 44 percent of those 65 years and older. They also found that most Minnesotans played the game rather regularly. About 31 percent bought tickets once a week or more, 23 percent bet on the lottery two or three times a month, and 46 percent wagered once a month or less. Finally, most Minnesotans (58 percent) felt positive about the lottery, while 36 percent were negative about it. (Six percent had no opinion.)

A NATIONAL LOTTERY

Thomas Jefferson, author of the Declaration of Independence and third president of the United States, thought "the lottery is a wonderful thing; it lays taxation only on the willing." Recent successes in state lotteries have inspired several Congressmen to introduce national lottery bills, but, to date, none have succeeded.

Some of the major arguments in support of a national lottery are: 1) it would be a voluntary method of raising money; 2) revenues, estimated at between $6 and $50 billion a year, could help reduce the national debt, bolster the nation's Social Security system, or supplement education and child welfare programs; 3) a lottery is no more regressive (in which a larger portion of revenue is taken from the poor than from middle- and upper-income groups) than sales taxes, which affect everyone equally, regardless of income; and 4) studies indicate that state-operated lotteries decrease activity in illegal numbers games.

Some of the major arguments against a national lottery are: 1) better methods of balancing the federal budget should be used; 2) lotteries are not productive revenue-raisers and would make only a small dent in the total national debt; 3) they are immoral, creating an environment where the "chance ethic" is more important than the "work ethic;" 4) they promote compulsive gambling; 5) they are a regressive form of taxation; 6) they contribute to organized crime; and 7) a national lottery would become a direct competitor to state lotteries.

Politically Unlikely

Probably the most important reason that a national lottery is unlikely is that it would draw money away from the state lotteries. The North American Association of State and Provincial Lotteries, a trade organization which represents the state and provincial lotteries in North America, strongly opposes a federal lottery and has vowed to fight it. They feel that it will not be hard for state lottery officials to lobby representatives and senators from their states and convince them that a national lottery would have a devastating impact on their state incomes. Furthermore, it is easier to convince voters that lottery money should help out at the state and local level rather than be sent to Washington, DC.

LOTTERIES - A WORLDWIDE PASSION

Lotteries are as popular in other parts of the world as they are in the United States and there are lottery games in countries on every continent. According to *Gaming and Wagering Business,* worldwide lottery sales (including the U.S.) in 1991 reached $71.6 billion, up 11 percent from $64.4 billion in 1990. Europe had the most lottery sales ($29.7 billion), followed by North America ($25.5 billion), Asia ($8.7 billion), Australia and New Zealand ($2.3 billion), Central and South America ($1.4 billion), and Africa ($440 million). By country, the United States sold the most lottery tickets ($20.5 billion), followed by Spain ($7.2 billion) and the Federal Republic of Germany ($7.2 billion), Japan ($5 billion), and Canada ($3.5 billion).

The largest lotteries in volume sales in 1991 were the Spanish National Lottery ($7.25 billion), Japan's Dai-ichi Kangyo Bank, Lottery Division ($5 billion), the French Lottery ($4.1 billion), the Italian National Lottery ($2.7 billion), the Florida Lottery ($2.1 billion).

CHAPTER VIII

ILLEGAL GAMBLING IN AMERICA

Illegal gambling, like legal gambling, is deeply rooted in American society. Despite innumerable federal and state laws and competition from state-supported legal gambling, illegal wagering remains a part of American life.

TYPES OF ILLEGAL GAMBLING

There are four principal forms of illegal gambling: 1) the numbers, 2) horsebooks (betting on horses), 3) sportsbooks (betting on sporting events), and 4) sportscards.

The Numbers Game

The forerunner of modern numbers gambling was a game called "policy." Policy was often a sideline game of the lotteries. Originally, lotteries were used to raise money for civic or charitable causes, while policy was played to earn money for the lottery company, since policy can be played more quickly than a lottery. It is commonly believed that the game of policy gave rise to gambling syndicates, which raised the large sums of money required to operate a policy shop.

Policy gambling radically changed when "numbers" was introduced as a separate and rival game. During the 1920s, African Americans were migrating from the rural South into northern cities. Policy and numbers appealed to members of poor African American communities and political organizations. During the 1930s, ex-bootleggers fought for control of black policy and numbers operations. Using their political connections and money gained from bootlegging, white mobsters

forced African-American policy and numbers operators to join with them or risk being put out of business — or worse. This conflict usually ended in a partnership, with the original owners staying on as managers and operators, and the mobsters providing such services as "protection," financial backing, regulation of competition, and legal representation in court when required.

How the Numbers Game is Played

To be successful, numbers games require the participation of a large volume of people. The bettor places his or her bet for any desired amount on a number from 000 to 999 and receives a receipt indicating the chosen number and the amount wagered. One digit numbers have an 8-to-1 payoff ($8 is won for every $1 wagered), two-digit numbers have a 60-70 to 1 payoff, and three-digit numbers pay 550-600 to 1.

The wager money is left with a "collector," (who often operates a numbers game as a sideline to a restaurant, candy store or drugstore, gas station, or another business that involves a lot of public contact). A "pickup man" collects the wagers from the collector and delivers them to the "bank," which is a central headquarters or processing center where the winning numbers are determined and payoffs are made, usually based on the results at a local racetrack. Usually, the collector does not know what bank the pickup man works for, so if a collector is arrested, the entire operation will not be jeopardized. Gross profit for the bank may be as high as 40 percent of the total amount wagered, but the administrative costs are also high. The net profit for numbers games is usually about 1 percent, and rarely exceeds 10 percent.

Numbers Is One of the Most Popular Forms of Illegal Gambling

Although illegal, most numbers operations take place openly while law enforcement officers may be paid to look the other way. In fact, numbers is often cited as a primary source of police corruption. When the occasional police raid does occur, numbers operators and their customers view them as a minor nuisance.

The game thrives in New York City's poor neighborhoods and is probably the most lucrative form of illegal gambling in the City. Some politicians and observers believe that the numbers racket is so deeply entrenched in the culture of poor neighborhoods that it has become part of the local economy. Recent immigrants and many poor people may not even know that the game is illegal and that it often supports organized crime.

Horsebooks — How a "Bookie" Operates

The bookmaker or "bookie" was first identified with the gambling business during the 1870s, when race tracks licensed them to accept bets. For that privilege, bookies paid the race track a daily fee, usually around $100 (a very large sum in those days). Once established, bookies branched out into (illegal) off-track betting parlors in the cities to provide services to bettors who could not attend races.

When placing a bet with a bookie, the bettor makes his or her choice from a scratch sheet that contains information on post (starting) times, post positions, a horse's lineage and past performance, expected odds, and handicappers' picks. The bookie pays off the same amount as the track, keeping the 15 percent normally charged by the track for himself. After expenses, the bookie will normally make a 10 to 11 percent net profit.

In order to have enough financial support to cover bets, bookies generally form syndicates. The syndicate gives each bookie the latest information about jockey changes, betting odds, and race track conditions.

Sportsbooks — The Most Popular Form of Illegal Gambling

While many forms of gambling in the U.S. have been legalized, gambling on sporting events continues to be illegal in all but four states and is legal statewide only in Nevada. Some sources estimate that professional football alone attracts $50 billion in wagers per season or possibly as much as $10 million per football weekend in major cities. This figure does not include wagers on college football games. According to Eugene M. Christensen of *Gaming and Wagering Business*, sports betting is the fastest growing type of illegal gambling. This has become especially true since with lotteries in most states, gamblers have an option of betting legally on the numbers.

The *Miller Lite Report on American Attitudes Toward Sports* (Milwaukee, WI, 1983) asked people how frequently they bet on professional sports competitions. Fifty-nine percent reported never betting, but about one out of every four persons said they bet either occasionally or frequently. Those betting most frequently are usually young to middle-aged males earning between $10,000 and $15,000 or over $25,000 per year. For both sports fans and non-fans alike, the overwhelming majority bet less than $100 per year on sporting events, but a small percentage place bets amounting to $500 and more during a year.

Radio and television contribute, perhaps inadvertently, to the huge amount of betting on sporting events. Most local newspapers make the point spreads readily available to the general public and it is not unusual for sportswriters and sportscasters to predict the outcome of a game and include the "point spread" (see below) in their predictions.

Many bettors consider the advice of these professionals before they call their bookie to make a bet.

The "Point Spread"

A sports bookie is literally playing both ends against the middle, hoping to come out on top. The line, or "point spread," is manipulated to keep the odds on the bookie's side. The 1/2 point spread is the device used in changing the line. A bookie must be careful not to change the spread too much or he might end up paying off both sides. Lines vary among bookmakers, and some bettors shop around for the spread that is most acceptable.

During the football season, the "early line" is posted every Tuesday in the legal sports books in Nevada. For example, in a game in which the Cleveland Browns are playing the Dallas Cowboys, the line might start at Dallas +6. This means that, for the Cowboy supporter, Dallas must win by 7 points for the bettor to win because 6 points will be subtracted from the Cowboys' final score. Both the legal line in Las Vegas and the illegal line created by the bookies fluctuate during the week, usually because of the bettor's interpretation of everything from changes in the weather to the condition of the players' health. Competent bookies, however, will only move the line in response to how much money is being bet on each team, not conjecture about players and weather.

A good bookie does not care who wins. He or she moves the point spread up or down in order to keep the betting even. If the line goes from Dallas +6 to Dallas +8, it is because that is what is needed to get more people to bet on Cleveland instead of Dallas. Normally, by the end of the week as the game approaches, the legal and illegal point spread will usually be very close, if not the same.

Today, most bookmaking operations are partnerships which employ several workers to record bets and compute the day's business. The bookmakers decide how to shift the point spread, when to lay off bets (get help from other bookies in covering bets), what limits to set for bets, and how much credit to extend to customers.

As with numbers games, illegal sports betting sometimes requires that law enforcement officials be unobservant. In order to avoid confrontations with the law, bookies use various methods to conceal their operations, such as frequently moving, using answering services, and changing telephone numbers.

Sportscards

Sportscards are very popular for the $1 to $10 sports bettor. Sportscards list a particular week's sporting events along with the point spreads. The cards are distributed no later than Tuesday for games which will take place the coming weekend. The bettor selects the team(s) he or she thinks will win, tears off the card stub and submits it to the bookie before the game takes place.

COLLEGE AND PRO SPORTS GAMBLING

College officials nationwide are expressing alarm at the phenomenal increase in betting on college sports. Many people feel that betting poses a threat to the integrity of the sports. "Point shaving" scandals (a player has been paid to deliberately score fewer points than he or she might have during a particular game) still occasionally surface. Basketball is considered the easiest game to "fix" because it is so easy to purposely miss shots without appearing to be doing so. A player on a team that is winning might easily rationalize missing a basket here and there in order to stay within a point spread — his team will win anyway and so, he thinks, neither team nor fans get hurt. A missed shot, however, can be very important to someone betting on a specific point spread.

The issue of point-spread sometimes comes up at the end of a football game when a team does something that appears to make little sense, for instance, when the losing team goes for a field goal when the game is far out of reach and the assured three points means little, or when a team that is leading by a wide margin goes for an extra touchdown. So far, however, there has never been any positive proof of point shaving in college or professional football.

Some observers feel that the pressure of sports events for both coaches and players is due, in part, to televised broadcasts of the games. With the growing popularity and availability of cable TV, the pressure could well become greater. According to a *Special Report on Gambling* published by *Sports Illustrated* in 1986, the National Football League (NFL) and the TV networks gloss over gambling.

The evidence is that in dealing with gambling, as with other problems such as cocaine use by players, abuse of anabolic steroids and artificial turf-related injuries, ... the National Football League seems especially inclined to gloss over gambling associations.... [Its] tolerant attitude toward gambling appears to be shared by the TV networks... [who] need full armchairs — people anchored in front of sets watching games [in other words, they need the ratings].

HOW MUCH MONEY IS BET ON ILLEGAL GAMBLING?

It is virtually impossible to estimate how much money is bet illegally in the United States. The last complete survey of American gambling behavior was done in 1975 for the Federal Commission on the Review of the National Policy Towards Gambling. Well over a decade and a half old, this study is of little value in the 1990s. The U.S. Treasury estimated the amount of illegal gambling from 1973-1981 (released in 1983), but gave up on a 1990 attempt to update their findings. The U.S. Treasury concluded that there was simply not enough reliable data available on which to make even a broad estimate.

Until their 1989 survey of gambling in America, *Gaming and Wagering Business* included an estimate of illegal gambling, but in 1990 dropped their estimate because:

No one — not the F.B.I., not Treasury, not Internal Revenue, or your local police department and certainly not your local newspaper — *knows* how much illegal gambling there is in the United States.

The absence of reliable statistics cannot be made up from the annual accumulation of anecdotal records: media reports of gambling arrests, more or less informed investigations by law enforcement and legislative agencies, telephone calls, conversations with more or less knowledgeable persons with an interest in the subject.

... Therefore, estimates of illegal gambling have been deleted from the 1991 installment of this series — not because illegal gambling does not exist, it does, but because there is no basis for making estimates. And there the matter will have to rest, unless and until new data become available. ("U.S. Gaming Handle up 14% in '90," Eugene M. Christiansen, *Gaming and Wagering Business*, July 15, 1991, August 14, 1991, p. 40.)

In their survey of gambling for 1989, *Gaming and Wagering Business*, based on earlier estimates and their own intuition, had estimated that Americans had illegally bet $43 billion — $8.1 billion on horsebooks, $27.4 billion on sports betting, $2.1 billion on sportscards, and $5.5 billion on numbers. Of the total $43 billion, *Gaming and Wagering Business* estimated that the house, either organized crime or individual bookies, kept about $6.7 billion - $2.8 billion from numbers, $1.4 billion from horsebooks, $1.2 billion from sportsbooks, and $1.3 billion from sportscards. *Forbes Magazine* has estimated illegal sports betting at $100 billion. These figures, however, represent little more than educated guesses.

In conclusion, Eugene Christiansen believes that, based on all accounts

illegal gambling is flourishing in this country. There is no reason to suppose the illegal games, except, perhaps, illegal numbers games that have to compete with well-run, extensively advertised state lottery numbers games, have suffered measurable declines — but there is no way to know. ("U.S. Gaming Handle up 14% in '90," Eugene M. Christiansen, *Gaming and Wagering Business*, July 15, 1991, August 14, 1991, p. 40.)

With the continued growth of amateur and professional sports in the United States, and the unlikelihood that legal sports gambling will extend beyond the states in which it is currently legal in some form or another (DE, NV, OR, MT, and possibly NJ), illegal sports betting will likely continue to grow and be the most important part of illegal gambling. (See Chapter II, Professional and Amateur Sports Protection Act of 1992.)

GAMBLING ARRESTS

Gambling is simply not a high priority with the nation's police. In 1982, police arrested 41,200 people for gambling. In 1987, they arrested 23,000. In 1990, police arrested only 19,300 and in 1992, only 17,100. This huge drop in the number of people arrested for gambling occurred during a time when the overall number of arrests was increasing. The 17,100 people arrested for gambling in 1992 were only 0.12 percent (that is less than one-eight of one percent) of all those arrested. More than five times as many people were arrested for curfew violations (91,100) and 14 times as many were arrested for weapons violations (239,300). With the increase in violent crime and drug-related crimes and the growth in legal gambling, gambling has become a low priority for the nation's police.

CHAPTER IX

PUBLIC OPINION ABOUT GAMBLING

In 1992, the Gallup Poll surveyed Americans to determine their attitudes towards gambling and the huge increase in legal gambling in just a few years. In 1989, when the Gallup researchers last surveyed the country on gambling, 29 states and the District of Columbia had introduced lotteries. Three years later, 35 states were offering their citizens the chance to win the lottery. Meanwhile, along the Mississippi River, in the states of Illinois, Iowa, and Mississippi, riverboat gambling had become legal. Casinos in Colorado and South Dakota are attracting hundreds of thousands of patrons and gambling casinos located on Native American reservations across the country are attracting many hundreds of thousands more.

A COOLING OFF TOWARDS GAMBLING?

The 1992 Gallup survey generally found what the researchers described as a "cooling off" in the nation's enthusiasm toward gambling. However, this might not necessarily mean the nation is cooling off towards gambling, it might just mean the country has reached the point of maximum support for gambling.

TABLE 9.1
*Opinion of Legal Gambling — Trend**

	Approve	Disapprove	No opinion
Bingo for cash prizes			
1992	72%	25%	3%
1989	75	23	2
1982	74	†	†
1975	68	†	†
Casino gambling at resort areas			
1992	51	47	2
1989	54	42	4
1982	51	†	†
1975	40	†	†
Casino gambling in a major city			
1992	40	57	3
Lotteries for cash prizes			
1992	75	24	1
1989	78	21	1
1982	72	†	†
1975	61	†	†
Offtrack betting on horse races			
1992	49	47	4
1989	54	42	4
1982	54	†	†
Betting on professional sports such as baseball, basketball, or football			
1992	33	65	2
1989	42	55	3
1982	51	†	†
1975	31	†	†
Casino gambling on Indian reservations			
1992	42	51	7
Casino gambling on so-called "river boats"			
1992	60	38	2

* 1975 data: University of Michigan
  1982 data: Gallup for Gaming Business Magazine
† Data not available

Source: The Gallup Poll, Princeton, NJ

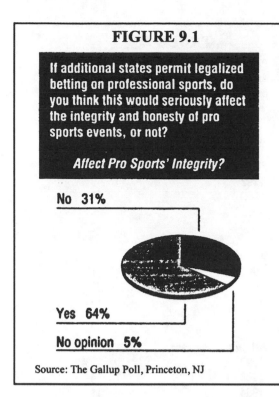

FIGURE 9.1

If additional states permit legalized betting on professional sports, do you think thi$ would seriously affect the integrity and honesty of pro sports events, or not?

Affect Pro Sports' Integrity?

No 31%

Yes 64%

No opinion 5%

Source: The Gallup Poll, Princeton, NJ

TABLE 9.2

I'd like to know whether you agree or disagree with each of the following arguments *in favor of* legalized state-sponsored gambling. First, do you agree or disagree that...(ROTATED)

Pro-gambling Arguments

	Agree	Disagree	No opinion
It provides much-needed revenue for programs such as education and senior citizens	57%	41%	2%
If the state sponsors gambling, organized crime can be kept out	37	59	4
It creates jobs and helps stimulate the local economy	64	33	3
People will gamble anyhow, so the state might as well make it legal and get some of the revenue	61	38	1

Now I'd like to know whether you agree or disagree with each of the following arguments *against* legalized gambling. First, do you agree or disagree that...(ROTATED)

Anti-gambling Arguments

	Agree	Disagree	No opinion
It encourages people who can least afford it to squander their money	64%	34%	2%
It is immoral	32	65	3
It can make compulsive gamblers out of people who would never participate in *illegal* gambling	58	40	2
It opens the door for organized crime	62	33	5

Source: The Gallup Poll, Princeton, NJ

The Gallup researchers asked those surveyed whether they approved or disapproved of various forms of gambling. About 72 percent said they approved of bingo for cash prizes, down from 75 percent in 1989, but still somewhat above the 68 percent of 1975. About half the country (51 percent) supported casino gambling at resort areas, down from 54 percent in 1989, but still well above the 40 percent in 1975. (See Table 9.1.)

On the other hand, only 40 percent approved of gambling in major cities as has been considered in cities such as New Orleans or Chicago. At the same time, Americans were more supportive of casino gambling on riverboats (60 percent). (See Table 9.1.)

Even support for the lotteries dropped somewhat from 78 percent in 1989 to 75 percent in 1992. Nonetheless, it is still well above the 61 percent who supported lotteries in 1975. Support for offtrack betting on horses fell from 54 percent in 1989 to 49 percent in 1992.

Americans definitely felt more uncomfortable with betting on professional sports such as base-ball, basketball, and football. In 1982, about half (51 percent) of those interviewed approved of such gambling. However, by the end of the decade, support had dropped to 42 percent and, in 1992, only one-third (33 percent) of Americans thought betting on sports was a good idea.

In fact, almost two-thirds (64 percent) thought that permitting legalized betting on professional sports would "seriously affect the integrity and honesty of pro sports events." (See Figure 9.1.) About half of all Americans (48 percent) thought that betting on National Football League (NFL) and National Basketball Association (NBA) should be banned all together. Only about one-third (33 percent) of those interviewed wanted to see sports betting extended beyond the states (Nevada, Oregon and New Jersey) where it is already legal or potentially legal.

ARGUMENTS SUPPORTING GAMBLING

Americans generally agree with the arguments supporting gambling, many of which are economic. Most Americans agreed that gambling "creates jobs and helps stimulate the local economy" (64 percent) and "provides much-needed revenue for programs such as education and senior citizens" (57 percent). (See Table 9.2.)

About 3 out of 5 people (61 percent) thought "people will gamble anyhow, so the state might as well make it legal and get some of the revenue." On the other hand, only 37 percent believed that "if the state sponsors gambling, organized crime can be kept out."

ARGUMENTS OPPOSING GAMBLING

At the same time that a majority agree with the arguments supporting gambling, a majority also agree with many of the arguments opposing gambling. Almost 2 out of every 3 Americans (64 percent) agreed that gambling "encourages people who can least afford it to squander their money." (See Table 9.2.) A similar proportion (62 percent) believed it "open[ed] the door for organized crime." Well over half (58 percent) thought gambling "can make compulsive gamblers out of people who would never participate in *illegal* gambling."

The moral argument, however, held little sway since barely one-third (32 percent) believed gambling was immoral. Protestants (41 percent) were more than twice as likely as Catholics (18 percent) to believe gambling was immoral. Among the various Protestant denominations, Southern Baptists (50 percent) were far more likely to believe gam-

TABLE 9.3

Please tell me whether or not you have done any of the following things in the past 12 months. First, how about...

Gambling Activities — Trend
(Based on those responding "yes")

Played bingo for money
1992	9%
1989	13
1982*	9
1950	12

Visited a casino
1992	21%
1989	20
1984	18
1982*	12

Bet on a horse race
1992	12%
1989	14
1984	11
1982*	9
1950	4
1938	10

Bought a state lottery ticket
1992	56%
1989	54
1982*	18

Bet on a professional sports event such as baseball, basketball, or football
1992	12%
1989	22
1984	17
1982*	15

Bet on a *college* sports event such as basketball or football
1992	6%
1989	14

Bet on a boxing match
1992	6%
1989	8

Participated in an office pool on the World Series, Superbowl or other game
1992	22%

* Gallup for Gaming Magazine

Source: The Gallup Poll, Princeton, NJ

bling was immoral than were the other Protestant denominations (29 percent).

HOW AMERICANS GAMBLE

The Gallup Poll found a significant decrease in how many people participated in most forms of gambling. The proportion who played bingo within the last year fell from 13 percent in 1989 to 9 percent in 1992. The percentage who bet on horse races dropped from 14 percent to 12 percent over the same period. (See Table 9.3.)

Betting on sporting events dropped sharply. The percentage betting on professional sports tumbled from 22 percent in 1989 to only 12 percent in 1992, while the proportion betting on college sports plummeted from 14 percent to 6 percent.

Only betting at a casino, which rose marginally from 20 percent in 1989 to 21 percent in 1992, and buying state lottery tickets, which increased from 54 percent to 56 percent during this time period, avoided a drop. This was most likely because it had become easier to buy a lottery ticket now that the number of states selling lottery tickets has increased from 29 to 36 over this period and the number of states with casinos has grown from only a few in 1989 to 27 that offered some form of casino gambling 1992. (See Table 9.3.)

Similar declines were noted in the frequency of gambling. While there was little change in gambling frequency among those visiting a casino, the percentage who bought lottery tickets once a week or more dropped from 23 percent to 19 percent. Apparently these people did not stop buying lottery tickets altogether since the proportion buying tickets monthly or less increased. (See Table 9.4.) At the same time the proportion betting weekly, monthly, or less often on professional sporting events dropped sharply while the percentage bet-

---

TABLE 9.4

How often do you [ITEM; ROTATED)...once a week or more often, 2 to 3 times a month, once a month, once every few months, or less often? (based on those who participated in last 12 months)

Gambling Frequency — Trend

	Weekly or more	Monthly Monthly	Less often	No opinion
Visit a casino				
1992	1%	2%	19%	0%
1989	1	1	18	1
Bet on a horse race				
1992	1	2	8	1
1989	1	3	10	•
Buy a state lottery ticket				
1992	19	20	16	1
1989	23	16	14	•
Bet on professional football when it's in season				
1992	5	3	4	•
1989	6	5	11	•

• Less than 0.5%

Source: The Gallup Poll, Princeton, NJ

TABLE 9.5

How much money do you usually spend each month on lottery tickets? (based on those who purchased ticket in last 12 months)

Monthly Expenditures on Lottery — Trend

	1989	1992
$30 or more	12%	9%
$20-29	11	11
$10-19	18	19
$5-9	24	17
$1-4	22	28
Less than $1	11	14
No opinion	2	2
	100%	100%
Mean	$53	$28
Median	$5	$5

Source: The Gallup Poll, Princeton, NJ

ting monthly or less often on horse racing also dropped.

Meanwhile, the average amount spent monthly on the lottery dropped from $53 in 1989 to only $28 in 1992. Most of the drop occurred among small bettors who wagered $5 to $9 in 1989, but who were more likely to bet $1 to $4 in 1992. (See Table 9.5.)

The economic recession of the early 1990s undoubtedly contributed to this decline, but the decline in enthusiasm for lotteries, which appears to come naturally after they have been around for a few years, also contributed to this drop. In addition, most observers believe that the increased availability of lotteries and casino gambling have contributed to the decline in betting on horse races and sporting events.

The fun has gone out of gambling for many people. The Gallup researchers found that while the proportion of Americans who enjoyed making bets "a lot" remained unchanged from 1989 to 1992 at 7 percent, the proportion who enjoyed gambling "a little" dropped from 27 percent to 22 percent over the same period. (See Table 9.6.) Meanwhile, the percentage who did not like betting at all rose from 38 percent to 45 percent. Perhaps the growth in the availability of gambling has reached the point where it has fulfilled the demand. In addition, many people who were not gamblers may have been attracted by the newness of a new lottery or new gambling casino, but after a while the novelty wore off.

A BREAKDOWN OF ATTITUDES TOWARDS GAMBLING

Table 9.7 shows the attitudes of Americans towards the various types of gambling by characteristics. The Gallup researchers found that, generally, no matter what the type of gambling, males will be more likely to favor the type of gambling than females (with the exception of bingo and sports betting), younger people are more likely to approve of gambling than older people, Southern-

TABLE 9.6

How much do you yourself enjoy making bets? Would you say you enjoy making bets a lot, a little, not too much or not at all?

Enjoy Gambling?

	1989	1992
A lot	7%	7%
A little	27	22
Not too	27	26
Not at all	38	45
No opinion	1	•
	100%	100%

• Less than 0.5%

Source: The Gallup Poll, Princeton, NJ

ers are less likely to support gambling than those from other regions, and those living in urban or suburban areas are more likely to favor gambling than those in rural areas.

Except for tribal gaming (gambling on Native American reservations), blacks are more likely than whites to approve of gambling; except for Off-Track Betting (OTB), those with no college were more likely to support gambling than those with some college education; Democrats and Independents were far more likely to favor gambling than Republicans; and Catholics were far more likely than Protestants to support gambling. Those Americans who considered religion very important were also less likely to approve of gambling than those who saw religion as less important in their lives.

BETTING ON SPORTS

Almost half (48 percent) of those surveyed by the Gallup Poll thought betting on professional sports should be banned altogether and 15 percent thought it should be limited to a few states as it is now. Only about one-third (33 percent) of those interviewed believed betting on professional sports should be expanded. (See Table 9.8.)

TABLE 9.7

Opinion On Several Types Of Legalized Gambling
(November 20-22, 1992; Survey GO 322034, Q. 2.)

QUESTION: As you may know, some states legalize betting so that the state can raise revenues. Please tell me whether you would approve or disapprove of legalizing each of the following types of betting in your state to help raise revenues. First, would you approve or disapprove of: Bingo for cash prizes; next, would you approve or disapprove of casino gambling at resort areas; casino gambling in a major city; lotteries for cash prizes; off-track betting on horse races; betting on professional sports such as baseball, basketball or football; casino gambling on Indian reservations; casino gambling on so-called "river boats." [ON ANY ITEM WHERE RESPONDENT REPLIED "ALREADY LEGAL," then asked:] Do you approve or disapprove of its being legal?

	Lotteries		Bingo		River boat		Resort areas	
	Approve	Disapprove	Approve	Disapprove	Approve	Disapprove	Approve	Disapprove
National	75%	24%	72%	25%	60%	38%	51%	47%
Sex								
Male	77	23	72	26	64	35	53	45
Female	74	24	73	24	57	40	49	49
Age								
18-29 years	85	15	85	13	72	27	66	34
30-49 years	80	19	74	24	63	35	53	46
50 and older	65	32	63	33	52	44	41	56
65 & older	62	34	63	30	49	46	39	58
Region								
East	85	14	77	19	67	30	60	38
Midwest	74	24	71	25	59	38	48	48
South	77	22	68	30	54	45	44	55
West	77	22	73	25	62	36	53	45
Community								
Urban	80	20	75	23	64	35	54	44
Suburban	75	24	72	24	61	38	52	46
Rural	69	27	69	29	54	41	45	53
Race								
White	74	24	72	25	60	38	50	48
Non-white	83	16	76	23	66	32	57	41
Education								
College	73	26	71	27	58	41	50	49
No college	77	21	73	23	62	35	51	46
Politics								
Republicans	65	33	62	35	50	48	43	56
Democrats	80	19	78	20	64	33	53	44
Independents	79	20	75	22	65	34	55	43
Income								
$50,000 & over	75	25	73	26	62	37	49	49
$30,000-49,999	80	19	74	24	67	33	59	40
$20,000-29,999	79	19	78	20	65	34	55	45
Under $20,000	72	26	70	26	54	40	44	52
Religion								
Protestant	70	28	67	30	55	42	43	54
Catholic	85	14	82	16	75	23	67	32
Importance of Religion								
Very	68	30	67	30	53	44	44	54
Fairly	86	14	80	18	71	28	60	39
Not important	88	11	84	13	72	27	64	33
Gambling behavior								
Non-gamblers	53	45	52	44	33	64	23	74
Bingo/lottery/ pools only	84	14	81	16	65	32	55	43
Sports/casino/ racetrack	89	11	84	15	81	18	73	26

Note: "No opinion" omitted.

(Continued on following page.)

TABLE 9.7 (Continued)

	O.T.B.		Tribal gaming		Major city casinos		Pro sports betting		No. of interviews
	Approve	Disapprove	Approve	Disapprove	Approve	Disapprove	Approve	Disapprove	
National	49%	47%	42%	51%	40%	57%	33%	65%	1007
Sex									
Male	55	43	47	48	45	53	33	65	505
Female	43	52	39	53	36	61	33	65	502
Age									
18-29 years	59	39	45	54	56	44	43	57	177
30-49 years	53	45	46	47	42	57	38	61	428
50 and older	39	55	38	52	30	64	23	73	384
65 & older	38	55	35	53	27	66	24	73	169
Region									
East	52	43	44	46	42	54	35	63	250
Midwest	47	50	43	52	42	54	26	73	273
South	45	52	35	57	41	57	31	68	292
West	53	44	51	45	37	61	42	54	192
Community									
Urban	52	46	43	51	43	54	39	59	344
Suburban	53	44	42	52	40	58	32	66	376
Rural	40	53	42	50	38	58	27	71	282
Race									
White	47	49	43	50	40	58	32	66	896
Non-white	60	38	42	54	49	48	43	56	103
Education									
College	52	47	40	54	36	63	31	68	528
No college	45	48	44	48	44	52	35	63	469
Politics									
Republicans	42	56	37	58	33	67	28	71	317
Democrats	51	45	46	46	42	53	37	61	315
Independents	52	44	44	49	44	53	34	64	375
Income									
$50,000 & over	53	44	44	51	37	61	36	63	243
$30,000-49,999	53	44	48	47	43	56	35	64	235
$20,000-29,999	55	43	45	49	49	50	36	63	187
Under $20,000	40	55	39	53	38	57	30	67	251
Religion									
Protestant	44	53	40	54	36	60	28	71	612
Catholic	56	39	52	40	48	51	41	58	262
Importance of Religion									
Very	42	53	38	55	35	62	27	71	583
Fairly	56	42	52	43	47	52	40	59	282
Not important	65	35	55	42	46	45	50	48	133
Gambling behavior									
Non-gamblers	25	69	25	70	20	76	18	79	333
Bingo/lottery/ pools only	55	43	45	47	46	51	32	66	318
Sports/casino/ racetrack	65	32	56	37	56	43	48	50	356

Source: The Gallup Poll, Princeton, NJ

TABLE 9.8

Sports Wagering: Attitudes, Behavior

(November 20-22, 1992; Survey GO 322034, Q.'s 5, 8e. & 10d.)

QUESTIONS: What is your opinion of legalized betting on professional sports, such as NFL football games and NBA basketball games — do you think it should be banned altogether, limited to a few states (as it is now), or allowed to expand into other states? Please tell me whether or not you have done any of the following things in the past 12 months...Bet on a professional sports event such as baseball, basketball, or football...

How often do you [bet on professional football when it's in season]...once a week or more often, 2 to 3 times a month, once a month, once every few months, or less often?

	Opinion			Pro sports bet in last year?	Frequency of football wagers			
	Ban	Limit	Expand	Yes	Weekly	Monthly	Less often	No. of interviews
National	**48%**	**15%**	**33%**	**12%**	**5%**	**3%**	**4%**	**1007**
Sex								
Male	46	16	35	20	8	5	7	505
Female	49	14	31	5	2	1	1	502
Age								
18-29 years	39	20	39	22	10	6	6	177
30-49 years	43	16	37	14	5	3	6	428
50 and older	59	13	24	6	2	1	2	384
65 & older	60	10	25	4	1	1	2	169
Region								
East	47	17	32	13	7	2	3	250
Midwest	55	14	26	12	6	2	4	273
South	50	13	33	13	4	3	6	292
West	38	18	40	12	2	4	6	192
Community								
Urban	44	16	37	19	8	4	7	344
Suburban	49	17	31	10	3	2	5	376
Rural	51	13	29	8	4	3	2	282
Race								
White	49	15	32	12	4	3	5	896
Non-white	42	15	40	15	9	1	5	103
Education								
College	48	19	28	15	5	3	6	528
No college	48	12	36	11	4	3	3	469
Politics								
Republicans	52	16	29	14	6	3	6	317
Democrats	45	13	37	13	4	4	5	315
Independents	47	16	32	11	4	3	4	375
Income								
$50,000 & over	43	20	35	14	3	4	7	243
$30,000-49,999	47	20	30	12	5	4	4	235
$20,000-29,999	47	13	37	15	7	2	5	187
Under $20,000	51	12	31	11	5	3	3	251
Religion								
Protestant	52	16	28	11	4	3	4	612
Catholic	44	13	38	15	6	4	4	262
Importance of Religion								
Very	55	13	29	10	4	2	3	583
Fairly	40	18	37	13	5	4	4	282
Not important	36	19	39	23	8	5	10	133
Gambling behavior								
Non-gamblers	63	13	18	0	-	-	-	333
Bingo/lottery/ pools only	53	14	29	0	-	-	-	318
Sports/casino/ racetrack	31	18	48	33	13	8	13	356

Note: "No opinion" omitted

Source: The Gallup Poll, Princeton, NJ

Older Americans 50 years of age and older (about 60 percent) were far more likely to want sports betting banned than younger people 18-29 years of age (39 percent). Midwesterners (55 percent) and Southerners (50 percent) were more likely to support a ban than were Westerners (38 percent). More whites (49 percent) wanted sports betting banned than non-whites (42 percent). More respondents earning less than $20,000 (51 percent) wanted a ban than those earning $50,000 and over (43 percent).

Protestants (52 percent) were more likely to support a ban than Catholics (44 percent). Those who believe religion is very important (55 percent) were far more likely to support a ban on sports betting than those for whom religion was not very important (36 percent). Not surprisingly, non-gamblers (63 percent) were far more likely to support a ban than were those who gambled on sports, casino gambling, or the racetrack (31 percent). (See Table 9.8.)

About 12 percent of those interviewed had bet on professional sports at least once in the last year. Men, young people, people living in the city, non-whites, those with some college education, those making $20,000 to $29,000 a year, Catholics, those for whom religion was not important, and those who bet on sports, at casinos, and at racetracks were most likely have placed a sports bet in the last year. (See Table 9.8.)

The Gallup surveyors asked specifically about betting on football games. About 5 percent of those surveyed bet at least once a week on football and another 3 percent wagered at least once a month. Men, young people, Easterners, those living in cities, non-whites, those earning $20,000-$29,000, and those who did not consider religion important were most likely to bet on a football game. Not surprisingly, those who said they gambled on sporting events, at casinos, and at the racetrack were the most likely to also bet on football. (See Table 9.8.)

TABLE 9.9

Do you sometimes gamble more than you think you should?

Gamble Too Much? — Trend

	1989	1992
Yes	10%	9%
No	90	91
	•	•
	100%	100%

• Less than 0.5%

Source: The Gallup Poll, Princeton, NJ

TABLE 9.10

Has gambling ever been a source of problems within your family?

Gambling Caused Family Problems? — Trend

	1989	1992
Yes	4%	5%
No	96	95
No opinion	•	1
	100%	100%

• Less than 0.5%

Source: The Gallup Poll, Princeton, NJ

PUBLIC ATTITUDES TOWARDS GAMING ON NATIVE AMERICAN RESERVATIONS

Americans generally support the development of gambling on Native American reservations. In October 1992, the Harris Poll surveyed 1,205 adults living in states other than Nevada and New Jersey. When asked, "How about gambling on Indian reservations: Do you think Indian reservations, which want to, should be allowed to have casino gambling on their land or not?", 68 percent thought they should be allowed, 28 percent believed they should not, and 4 percent were not sure.

In August 1992, Dr. Bruce D. Merrill, Director of the Cactus State Poll, and the Media Research Program at Arizona State University polled 554 adults in the State of Washington on their attitudes towards gambling. They found that 62 percent supported gambling on Native American reservations, 26 percent opposed it, and 12 percent had no opinion. When supporters were asked why they favored gambling on Native American reservations, 42 percent indicated economic reasons: employment, jobs, money for the reservation, and reducing welfare, while 39 percent cited tribal sovereignty with comments such as "it's their land," "it's up to them," and "they should decide for themselves."

In November 1992, the Field Research Corporation surveyed 554 Californians on gambling on Native American reservations. Seventy-five percent supported lottery games on the reservations, 62 percent approved of slot machines, and 63 percent supported roulette. Twenty-eight percent of the supporters thought it would help Native Americans, 26 percent believed it would provide money for health, education, and welfare, 12 percent indicated it was "the only way Native Americans can earn money," and 11 percent believed Native Americans "should be able to use their land any way they want."

TABLE 9.11

TYPES OF GAMBLING EVER DONE

| | Total % | Gender | | Age | | | |
		Male %	Female %	18-34 %	35-49 %	50-64 %	65+ %
Played the lottery	82	85	80	82	88	84	70
Played slot machines, poker machines or other gambling machines	75	79	72	72	81	78	72
Gambled in a casino (legal or otherwise)	74	79	70	67	82	81	69
Bet on horses, dogs or other animals (at OTB, the track or with a bookie)	50	57	43	44	55	58	43
Played cards for money	44	59	31	48	46	42	37
Played bingo for money	34	28	40	25	39	37	39
Played the numbers	31	35	28	30	32	28	35
Played scratch off games other than lotteries	31	34	28	38	27	30	23
Bet on sports (parlay cards, with a bookie, or at Jai Alai)	26	41	13	34	26	24	13
Bowled, shot pool, played golf or some other game of skill for money	25	38	12	32	22	25	12
Played the stock, options and/or commodities market	24	30	20	21	29	30	17
Played dice games (including craps, over and under or other dice games) for money	19	30	8	20	18	20	15

Source: *New Jersey Residents' Attitudes and Behavior Regarding Gambling*, prepared by the Gallup Organization, Inc., for The Council on Compulsive Gambling of New Jersey, Inc. (Princeton, NJ, 1993)

DOES GAMBLING CAUSE PROBLEMS?

The Gallup researchers asked the respondents, "Do you sometimes gamble more than you think you should?" About 9 percent, virtually unchanged from the 10 percent of 1989, thought they gambled too much. (See Table 9.9.) When asked whether "gambling [has] ever been a source of problems within your family?" 5 percent indicated that it had, about the same as the 4 percent in 1989. (See Table 9.10.)

THE COUNCIL ON COMPULSIVE GAMBLING OF NEW JERSEY SURVEY

The Council on Compulsive Gambling of New Jersey, Inc. is aware that, for some people, gambling can cause grave problems. The Council asked the Gallup Organization (the Gallup Poll) of Princeton, NJ to study the "New Jersey resident's behavior and attitudes related to gambling." The Gallup Organization surveyed 1,016 adults to produce *New Jersey Residents' Attitudes and behavior Regarding Gambling* (Trenton, NJ, 1993).

The survey found that almost all (96 percent) New Jersey residents had gambled at some time during their lives. Most had played the lottery (82 percent), played slot machines (75 percent), or gambled in a casino (74 percent). This should not be surprising in a state that has a lottery and a major gambling center. About half (50 percent) had bet on the horse or dogs and significant percentages had played cards for money (44 percent), bingo for money (34 percent), and the numbers (31 percent). (See Table 9.11.)

Among those who gambled, 40 percent played the lottery at least once a week, 31 percent played the numbers at least once a week, 19 percent bowled, shot pool, or played golf for money at least

once a week, and 11 percent played cards for money at least once a week. (See Table 9.12.)

The Largest Amount Ever Gambled

The Gallup surveyors asked what was the largest amount the respondent had ever gambled. The average largest amount ever gambled was $403, although most (53 percent) had never gambled more than $100. About 8 percent had gambled $1000 or more at one time. (See Table 9.13.)

Getting Hooked

When asked how often they went back to win lost money, 80 percent said they never did. How-

TABLE 9.12

FREQUENCY OF PLAYING WITHIN PAST 12 MONTHS

(Based on those who have ever gambled)

	Once a Week Or More %	Less Than Once A Week %	Not At All/DK %
Played the lottery	40	45	15
Played slot machines, poker machines or other gambling machines	4	45	51
Gambled in a casino (legal or otherwise)	4	51	45
Bet on horses, dogs or other animals at OTB, the track or with a bookie	5	29	66
Played cards for money	11	33	56
Played bingo for money	8	24	68
Played the numbers	31	32	37
Scratch off games other than lotteries	11	48	41
Bet on sports (parlay cards, with a bookie, or at Jai Alai)	15	49	36
Bowled, shot pool, played golf or some other game of skill for money	19	37	44
Played the stock, options and/ or commodities market	18	42	40
Played dice games (including craps, over and under or other dice games) for money	5	40	55

Source: *New Jersey Residents' Attitudes and Behavior Regarding Gambling*, prepared by the Gallup Organization, Inc., for The Council on Compulsive Gambling of New Jersey, Inc. (Princeton, NJ, 1993)

ever, 16 percent said they did some of the time, 3 percent most of the time, and 1 percent every time. When asked, "Have you ever gambled more than you intended to?", 77 percent said no and 23 percent said yes. Men (28 percent) were more likely to have gambled more than they intended than women (18 percent). (See Table 9.14.) Younger people were more likely to gamble more than they intended than were older people.

About 5 percent said they would like to stop gambling, but could not. Eight percent of men, compared to 2 percent of women, would have liked to have stopped gambling, but could not. About 3 percent of those interviewed saw gambling as a way to escape their problems.

Do You Know Anyone with a Gambling Problem?

TABLE 9.13

LARGEST AMOUNT EVER GAMBLED

	Total %	Men %	Women %
Under $10	14	11	17
$10-49	26	20	32
$50-99	13	12	13
$100-149	15	15	16
$150-199	1	2	1
$200-249	8	11	5
$250-299	*	*	*
$300-399	3	3	2
$400-499	2	2	1
$500-599	4	6	3
$600-999	1	1	*
$1,000 or more	8	13	4
Don't know	5	4	6
Total	100	100	100
MEAN	$403	$594	$219
Number of Interviews	(976)	(504)	(472)

*Less than one-half of one percent.

Source: *New Jersey Residents' Attitudes and Behavior Regarding Gambling*, prepared by the Gallup Organization, Inc., for The Council on Compulsive Gambling of New Jersey, Inc. (Princeton, NJ, 1993)

When asked if they knew anyone who now had, or did have, a gambling problem, three-quarters (76 percent) did not know anyone. Fourteen percent knew a friend and 13 percent knew a relative. The father of 3 percent and the spouse of 2 percent had a problem. (See Table 9.15.) About 4 percent said that gambling, either by the respondent or a member of the family, had made his or her home life unhappy. When asked whether they knew anyone who gambled too much (but did not necessarily have a gambling "problem"), 28 percent said they knew someone with such a problem.

Who Should Provide Assistance to Compulsive Gamblers?

Most New Jerseyites believed that the state and the legal gambling companies should contribute to educate state residents about gambling and help treat compulsive gamblers. A large majority (78 percent) thought the state should provide education programs to students. A smaller majority (58 percent) believed the state should provide funding for treatment of compulsive gamblers. Almost three-fourths (72 percent) agreed that gambling companies should provide financial support for gambling programs.

Attitudes Towards Legal Gambling

The New Jersey study found that while most residents did not think gambling was illegal, most did believe that gambling entailed risks to society. Only 22 percent of those interviewed believed that gambling was immoral. Those over age 65 (30 percent) and those earning less than $25,000 (28 percent) were most likely to believe gambling was immoral. (See Table 9.16.)

However, 66 percent thought gambling "encourag[ed] people who can least afford it to spend money gambling," 57 percent agreed that gambling "can make compulsive gamblers out of people who would never participate in illegal gambling," 61 percent thought it "open[ed] the door for organized crime," and 59 percent thought that "gambling can erode young people's work ethics." The respondents were evenly split on whether "gambling teaches children that one can get something for nothing" with 49 percent agreeing and 48 percent disagreeing.

TABLE 9.14

FREQUENCY OF GOING BACK TO WIN LOST MONEY

		Gender		Household Income		
	Total %	Male %	Female %	<$25K %	$25K-$39.9 %	$40K+ %
Never	80	75	85	76	77	83
Some of the time	16	20	13	18	19	14
Most of the time	3	3	1	4	2	2
Every time	1	2	1	2	2	1
Don't know/Refused	*	*	0	0	0	*
Total	100	100	100	100	100	100
Number of Interviews	(976)	(504)	(472)	(290)	(208)	(398)

*Less than one-half of one percent.

TABLE 9.15

PEOPLE IN LIFE WHO HAVE GAMBLING PROBLEM

		Gender	
	Total %	Male %	Female %
Relative (NET)	13	12	14
Spouse	2	*	3
Father	3	3	3
Mother	1	1	1
Brother or sister	2	2	2
Children	*	*	*
Another relative	7	6	7
A friend	14	17	10
No one	76	74	78
Don't know/Refused	*	*	*
Number of Interviews	(1016)	(515)	(501)

*Less than one-half of one percent.

Source of above tables: *New Jersey Residents' Attitudes and Behavior Regarding Gambling*, prepared by the Gallup Organization, Inc., for The Council on Compulsive Gambling of New Jersey, Inc. (Princeton, NJ, 1993)

Where Do You Go for Help?

The researchers asked the New Jerseyites if they knew where to go for help. About half (48 percent) claimed they knew where to go for help and half (52 percent) did not. Among those who did know where to go, most (38 percent) indicated Gamblers Anonymous. Another 18 percent would go to the telephone book. About 12 percent would call 1-800-Gambler, the helpline set up by the Council on Compulsive Gambling of New Jersey, Inc. to assist those addicted to gambling. (See Table 9.17.)

TABLE 9.16

AGREEMENT WITH STATEMENTS

- Is immoral -

| | | Age | | | | Household Income | | |
	Total %	18-34 %	35-49 %	50-64 %	65+ %	<$25K %	$25K-$39.9 %	$40K+ %
Agree	22	20	21	20	30	28	25	17
Disagree	75	78	78	80	62	68	73	81
Don't know/Refused	3	2	1	1	8	4	2	2
Total	100	100	100	100	100	100	100	100
Number of Interviews	(1016)	(351)	(314)	(190)	(155)	(307)	(216)	(408)

TABLE 9.17

PLACE WOULD GO TO FIND HELP

All Who Say They Know Where to Find Help

| | | Age | | | | Household Income | | |
	Total %	18-34 %	35-49 %	50-64 %	65+ %	<$25K %	$25K-$39.9 %	$40K+ %
Gamblers Anonymous	38	31	42	43	33	31	35	42
1-800-Gambler	12	20	11	6	7	14	12	13
Hotline	8	8	6	11	5	5	12	8
Telephone book	18	23	12	15	21	18	25	12
Private doctor (Psychologist, Psychiatrist, etc.)	2	1	3	2	0	0	1	4
Through employer sponsored programs	2	1	2	2	2	0	1	3
Friends/family	2	2	3	1	3	4	0	2
Through county/state offices	5	1	8	5	11	9	4	4
Counseling centers (unspecified)	2	2	1	4	2	0	2	2
Other	4	4	2	2	6	7	3	2
Don't know/Refused	5	5	3	5	8	6	3	4
Number of Interviews	(492)	(163)	(158)	(109)	(58)	(116)	(114)	(217)

Source of both tables: *New Jersey Residents' Attitudes and Behavior Regarding Gambling*, prepared by the Gallup Organization, Inc., for The Council on Compulsive Gambling of New Jersey, Inc. (Princeton, NJ, 1993)

CHAPTER X

THE LOTTERY IS A GOOD IDEA

PREPARED STATEMENT BY DR. MARCIA LYNN WHICKER, PROFESSOR OF PUBLIC ADMINISTRATION, AND DR. TODD W. ARESON, ASSISTANT DIRECTOR OF CENTER FOR PUBLIC AFFAIRS, SCHOOL OF COMMUNITY AND PUBLIC AFFAIRS, VIRGINIA COMMONWEALTH UNIVERSITY, DECEMBER 10, 1987. (THIS STATEMENT REFLECTS THE VIEWS OF THE AUTHORS AND NOT NECESSARILY OF THE VCU ADMINISTRATION .)

LOTTERIES AS A METHOD OF RAISING GOVERNMENT REVENUES

While the lottery is pushed by supporters as a method of raising revenues for government without raising taxes, how lucrative is it? Where they exist, lotteries account for only a small percentage of state funding, typically two to four percent. Yet even a small percent can lead to substantial dollar amounts in larger states.

Lotteries have several pros and cons. Typically they are opposed by religious groups, which contend gambling is sinful. Supporters counter that churches themselves use "ungodly" gambling in the forms of bingo and raffles to raise revenues.

Critics argue that state lotteries encourage gambling and feed gambling addictions. Supporters argue that Americans are going to gamble anyway, and do so in the form of office pools, betting on professional football and basketball games, and illegal numbers games. Better, they say, that gambling proceeds be used to support desirable public purposes, such as education, medical care for the indigent, or services for the elderly, than to serve illegal ends.

Critics also argue that administrative costs for lotteries may run high relative to other taxes. Overhead for lotteries may run 15%, while the overhead on the general sales tax is as low as 2 to 5%. Supporters counter that comparing the lottery to taxes is unfair since it is not a tax. When viewed as a service, and compared to the costs of producing other types of entertainment, the yield for lotteries is high. The question of earmarking lottery revenues for special purposes is also controversial. While tying lottery proceeds to popular causes makes lottery adoption more politically palatable, critics contend that it hamstrings future budget decisions in the legislature and may result in funds being spent for purposes after the need has disappeared.

Perhaps the greatest criticism of the lottery, however, is that it is regressive, placing the greatest burden upon the poor, who buy more lottery tickets than the middle class or the rich. A 1975 study of the Connecticut, Massachusetts, and Pennsylvania lotteries examined the annual expenditure per family in those states. While the average expenditure in absolute dollars was greatest for middle income families, expenditures, as a percent of family income, were greater for low income families. This supports the notion that the impact of lotteries is regressive. Proponents, however, maintain that the lottery must be evaluated against

98

the regressivity of its alternatives. Other types of consumption taxes, especially the general sales tax, are equally regressive. Furthermore, a 1983 study of the Washington state lottery found that playing games there was growing in popularity with middle income citizens.

Despite its disadvantages, governments . . . have found lotteries an acceptable method of raising revenue. While states run government- sponsored lotteries in the U.S., Britain conducts national lotteries. There, horse-racing and bingo are two popular forms of lotteries. With recent mandates to government to do more with less, and increasing pressure on politicians not to raise taxes, nationwide, the lottery is an idea that just won't go away.

TESTIMONY OF MARTIN M. PUNCKE, DIRECTOR MARYLAND STATE LOTTERY, AND PRESIDENT NORTH-AMERICAN ASSOCIATION OF STATE LOTTERIES BEFORE THE COMMITTEE ON GOVERNMENTAL AFFAIRS, UNITED STATES SENATE, OCTOBER 3, 1984.

I believe a legal lottery is an appropriate function of State government providing the lottery was legally formed by the State legislature or was initiated by public referendum and approved by the general population of the State. The lottery then becomes a legal entity of the State and should be accepted and supported as such. I further believe that this type of revenue has proven to be a dependable revenue source and should be allowed to operate by the State without infringement by any other level of government. States should have the primary responsibility for determining what forms of gambling may legally take place within their boundaries.

A regressive tax is a tax which is applied to the entire population equally regardless of the financial status of any individual, thereby taking a larger percentage of the income from a low income group in proportion to a higher income group.

Several studies conducted by various authorities, most recently by Gallup in New Jersey, clearly and consistently verify the fact that lower income persons do not play the lottery in a greater proportion than their income group is in proportion to the general population.

No one is required to play the lottery, it is strictly voluntary. It is a consumer product which competes in the free marketplace, and has prospered and grown. Because of that success, lottery States have more nontax money for general public services. It is difficult to find a definition of the word "regressive" as used by lottery critics. In most cases, it appears to mean that it costs a person with a low income a higher percentage of his dollars to buy an item than it does for a person of a higher income. If the definition is accepted, there are very few things — the notable one being the progressive income tax — for which the critical definition of "regressive" does not apply.

We are all aware that the most regressive form of taxation is the sales tax because it is levied without regard for an individual income level and the poor pay a disproportionate amount of their income toward such a tax. A tax is compulsory while the purchase of a lottery ticket is discretionary.

TESTIMONY OF DANIEL W. BOWER, PRESIDENT, SCIENTIFIC GAMES, INC., BEFORE THE COMMITTEE ON GOVERNMENTAL AFFAIRS, UNITED STATES SENATE, OCTOBER 3, 1984.

ECONOMIC BENEFITS FROM A STATE LOTTERY

Probably the most dominant question asked about a lottery is how much revenue it can raise for a state. We have collected substantial information about lottery sales over the years. It is amazing to realize that gross revenues from United States lotteries have increased from $40 million in 1970 to over $6 billion in 1983! We have also been asked over the years to predict how much lottery revenues would be generated by a specific state. Consistently, our projections have been accurate, albeit sightly conservative.

Myths about a state lottery.

a. Lotteries and the poor.

Perhaps the most repeated objection to state operated lotteries is that poor people buy a disproportionate amount of lottery tickets. Some people take offense at objections to lotteries on this ground because, as Mayor Ernest Morial of New Orleans once said "The argument smacks of a kind of elitist paternalism that I find distasteful." In any event, the attack is totally unsubstantiated. Numerous detailed statistical studies have been done about the demographic characteristics of lottery players. These studies establish that lower income people play the lottery to a lesser degree than their proportion of the population. Typically, most lottery tickets are bought by persons between the ages of 35 and 54 whose household incomes are between $12,000 and $36,000. A related argument is that lotteries are a "regressive tax." However, a lottery is not a tax. It is an entirely voluntary activity on which people spend their discretionary income. Lotteries are no more a regressive tax than are movies, attendance at sports games, or any of the other numerous leisure time activities which people voluntarily decide whether to spend money on.

b. Lotteries and crime.

An objection that occasionally emerges is that lotteries create a law enforcement problem. Perhaps this objection finds it's origin in the lottery scandals of the early 1800s when lotteries were operated by private companies. Or, perhaps this objection finds its origin in preconceived prejudices about lotteries based on perceptions of what occur in the privately operated gaming industries of horse racing and casinos. Whatever the source of the objection, the objection itself is totally unfounded. Twenty years of experience with modern state lotteries has established conclusively that lotteries do not encourage crime and, in fact, quite the reverse is probably true. Even in California where opposition by public officials to lotteries has been the norm, a 1971 Task Force Report on Legalized Gambling for the Attorney General of California concluded that "the law enforcement problems attending state operated lotteries are minimal to nonexistent." Indeed, a national study commissioned by President Ford in 1975 reached this conclusion: "The presence of a state lottery decreased illegal gambling and accounts for a difference of almost 5 percentage points compared to a situation without a lottery. Since average participation in illegal gambling involves less than 11 % of the population, this is a substantial swing in behavior."

c. Compulsive gambling.

Occasionally, certain individuals associated with the treatment of compulsive gambling allege that lotteries create compulsive gamblers. These same people argue that a portion of the revenues from the sale of lottery tickets should be spent on compulsive gambling treatment centers. However, there is no factual basis to this claim. Even Monsignor Joseph Dunn, the President of the National Council on Compulsive Gambling, admits that there is "no acceptable research" done to establish that state operated lotteries cause compulsive gambling. In fact, a study by the Colorado State Lottery concluded that "lottery games, in general, do not appeal to persons whose compulsive behavior evidences itself in gambling or risktaking on a compulsive basis."

Newsweek reached a similar conclusion: "The only games that apparently pose no real threat of addiction are state lotteries. That's because they don't have enough action ." (*Newsweek*, March 3, 1980, page 70.)

d. Lotteries and the pari-mutuel industry.

Where there are established race tracks, the introduction of a state operated lottery occasionally is opposed by the pari-mutuel industry. There seems to be a "kneejerk" reaction that there is some phenomenon called "the gambling dollar" and that every dollar spent playing the lottery is one less dollar spent on pari-mutuel wagering. That position has never been supported by any empirical analysis which could be found and all available evidence indicates that it is simply untrue. In fact, in established lottery states, there has developed a very cooperative and mutually supportive relationship between the lottery and race tracks. We have investigated this situation and prepared a paper summarizing our results.

Conclusion

Lotteries are a tremendously popular and painless source of revenue. A survey by the University of Michigan, done in 1975 for the National Commission on Gambling, showed that 82% of the residents of lottery states approve of lotteries. Nationwide, the figure for approval is 71%. A more recent University of Michigan study found that public support for gaming increased dramatically in America between the date of their first survey and 1982.

CHAPTER XI

THE LOTTERY IS A BAD IDEA

TESTIMONY OF GERARD FULCHER ON BEHALF OF THE DELAWARE STATE GAMING COMMISSION BEFORE THE SENATE COMMITTEE ON GOVERNMENTAL AFFAIRS, OCTOBER 3, 1984

They say State lotteries will make a prolific amount of money for the State. They say virtually everyone is gambling anyway, so why not channel it legally. They say that lotteries are supported by a broad spectrum of people who will bet a little bit of money. They say that it decreased illegal gambling. They say there is no connection with crime, and they say there is no relationship to compulsive gambling.

Let's talk about profits, let's talk about what they call profits. They will tell you to measure the amount taken in, subtract the money you give to win, and subtract the overhead, subtract the money you give back to agents for being the middle man in this operation, and that is what they would like to label as profit.

But you have got to do a lot more subtracting. If they want to consider this as a business, then you subtract all the costs related to that business. That means you have to subtract the dollars and cents cost of criminal activity directly related to lotteries, and we know there have been many; a 30 percent increase in bad checks cashed in areas directly due to lotteries, in certain areas that were surveyed. We have the corruption that has been tied to the lotteries in several States, including a television person and a lottery official in Pennsylvania, indicted, convicted, and jailed, and on and on and on, the criminal activities that are directly related to that crime.

Lotteries do not raise terrific amounts of money when you subtract all of the costs involved. In order to perpetuate their bureaucracy, they have had to create a new clientele of gamblers to partake in their venture on a regular basis. The State has literally had to create new gamblers. Our study shows that 12 percent of the people who play the lottery regularly, and we estimate regularly to be three or more times a week, (12 percent of them) virtually never gambled before it was legalized. So one of their basic premises, that they are just giving the people already gambling an opportunity to do it legally, is a false premise.

TESTIMONY OF DR. LARRY BRAIDFOOT, GENERAL COUNSEL, THE CHRISTIAN LIFE COMMISSION, SOUTHERN BAPTIST CONVENTION, NASHVILLE, TENNESSEE, EXCERPTED FROM THE PAMPHLET, "STATE OPERATED LOTTERIES"

WHAT WILL A LEGALIZED LOTTERY DO?

The current drive to legalize state-operated lotteries has grown out of the increasing demands upon state budgets. State legislatures are looking for funds to meet the budget crises of the 1980's. Increasing taxes is never a popular thing for lawmakers to do.

Those who favor legalizing state lotteries usually present the following argument. The state needs more money. Increasing taxes is not popular; therefore, it is wise to consider some form of "taxation" which is voluntary. People are going to gamble, the argument continues. So it makes sense to legalize the gambling and to get some needed revenue for the states. This will have the additional benefit of pulling money away from illegal gambling which produces revenue for organized crime.

WHAT A LEGALIZED LOTTERY WILL REALLY DO

State-operated lotteries appeal dramatically to the poorest citizens of the state. There can be no reasonable doubt that the daily numbers game, the one upon which most of the state operated lotteries depend for their main source of revenue, appeals primarily to the poor and to the minority members of our society. Its appeal is based on the illusory promise and the desperate hope of a big win.

Daniel W. Bower is president and co-founder of Scientific Games, a corporation which specializes in lottery products and services. According to Bower, the "player selection" or numbers game attracts low-income minority players. The usual player is a laborer or service worker who is non-white, male, and has less than an eighth grade education. None of the lottery games has a strong appeal to middle-income and upper-income persons. . . . There can be no doubt, . . . that the most popular and lucrative lottery game is both targeted at and draws primarily from poor people.

Other studies confirm the candid admission of Bowers which was made at the Fourth Annual Gambling Conference and International Gaming Congress in 1982. Mark Abrahamson, a sociology professor at the University of Connecticut, reported to Connecticut's gaming commission that its daily lottery "primarily attracts poor, longterm unemployed and less educated participants." Daniel B. Suits, an economics professor at Michigan State University, has pointed out on several occasions that low-income lottery players wager a disproportionately high percentage of their income on the lottery. . . . Perhaps the most conclusive evidence of the manner in which lotteries appeal to poor people is the fact that their outlets are concentrated in poorer neighborhoods. One highly informative study was done in New Castle County, Delaware, in 1979. The study found no lottery outlets in the upper-income neighborhoods where 17,630 persons lived. There was one lottery outlet for every 17,774 persons in upper-middle income neighborhoods. There was one lottery outlet for every 5,032 persons in the lower-middle to middle-income neighborhoods. There was one lottery outlet for every 1,981 persons in the poorest neighborhoods.

STATE-OPERATED LOTTERIES ARE A REGRESSIVE AND INEFFICIENT WAY TO RAISE TAXES

A form of taxation is regressive if it draws a larger percentage of its revenue from the poorer citizens than from middle- and upper-class citizens. It is regressive if a poorer person spends a higher percentage of his or her income on the activity than does the person of modest or affluent means. Such is clearly the case with the lottery.

STATES WHICH SEEK TO RESOLVE THEIR FISCAL WOES BY LEGALIZING GAMBLING ACHIEVE MINIMAL SUCCESS

Revenues from gambling amount to little more than a patch on a state's financial woes. Of the 17 states which had legalized state lotteries by the end of 1983, all but three of the states already had legalized pari-mutuel gambling, three also had sports betting, off-track betting, and jai-alai, and two had casinos. . . Once states begin turning to legalized gambling for a source of revenue, the temptation builds to fix other financial woes by legalizing additional forms of gambling. Rather than bringing fiscal responsibility, the tendency is established to seek easy solutions to difficult financial problems. Most legalized gambling ventures generate much less than the amounts projected prior to legalization. A leading proponent of legalized lotteries claims that lotteries generate between one and four percent of the state revenues in those states where they are legal. Even if this is true, this is a very small percent of a state's budget.

STATE-OPERATED LOTTERIES DO NOT SUCCESSFULLY ELIMINATE OR REDUCE ILLEGAL GAMBLING.

One of the arguments made by lottery advocates is that the legalization of lotteries will persuade many individuals who currently bet in illegal games to switch to the legal game. Whether or not some of the players actually switch is uncertain. What is clear, however, is that there is no significant decrease in illegal gambling and illegal numbers games flourish alongside legal lotteries. Legal lotteries do not compete very well with the illegal games. Even pro-gambling leaders recognize this. There are several reasons. The illegal games have lower operating overhead and thus make higher payouts than the legal games. Operators of the illegal games give credit, enabling people to make bets even though they do not have the money to place the bet. And since illegal gambling winnings are not reported to the IRS, they, in effect, are not subject to taxes in the unlikely event of a significant win. Given those differences, if you were a gambler, where would you place your bet?

LEGALIZING GAMBLING IS A MORAL ISSUE

The decision to legalize gambling is a moral issue:

Pro-gambling forces advocate a morality which essentially justifies the gambling (the means) by the revenue it produces (the end). This is one type of morality. Another type . . . is a materialistic morality which longs for the opportunity of getting something for nothing, for the chance of being able to "get rich quick" apart from labor or the creation of a product of real value.

It is a moral issue when the state decides to derive income from an activity which is a regressive form of taxation that affects poor people more extensively than affluent people. It is a moral issue when a state decides not only to tolerate gambling but to get in the business of planning games, engaging in promotional activities (radio, television, newspapers, billboards), and targeting its citizens through extensive marketing analyses in the hopes of creating new gamblers to contribute taxes through and inefficient form of "tax farming."

It is a moral issue when a state adopts a form of gambling which in all probability will increase the extent and the amount of illegal gambling. It is a moral issue when a state adopts a form of gambling that will draw off large amounts of money especially from the poor people for whom the state supposedly has a responsibility to provide assistance.

PREPARED STATEMENT OF STATE REPRESENTATIVE JERRY KOPEL (CO) DECEMBER 23, 1987

Often players become bored with "numbers" the next game will likely be cable-TV play at-home, or electronic poker, with no skill involved. Escalation knows no ceiling. Big jackpots will always get bigger, and states will merge games across the borders. But the discretionary income needed to feed the lottery cannot grow as fast. Some other business will always lose the dollar that is diverted to lottery; someone doesn't buy a straw hat, or a necktie, or go to a movie.

Lottery is a state monopoly, and the state uses its gaming proceeds to urge residents to place their bets, stressing the pleasures gained from winning, and downplaying the horrendous odds of winning. The advertising appeal is answered by those who often dream of getting rich, the ones who have the least money. Studies by independent surveys (non-lottery funded) show that the poor spend more of their net income for lottery than do any other group.

And the state creates new gamblers where none existed, especially when the game duplicates the illegal numbers game.

Courts and law enforcement officials get a mixed message from lottery ads and lottery escalation. In most states, an individual doing what the state is doing would commit a felony and spend time in state prison. This makes it harder to get serious about prosecuting people who use the state's daily announced "number" for an illegal numbers game that pays more money to a bettor than does the state-run game.

Lottery proponents don't like to hear the lottery called a tax, but most impartial economists recognize it as such because of the transfer of income from an individual to the state. As a way of financing government, it is the least efficient with extremely high overhead costs compared to other tax collections. If history is any guide, the lottery is a fad that will eventually fade. States that don't adopt one will end up healthier for not doing so.

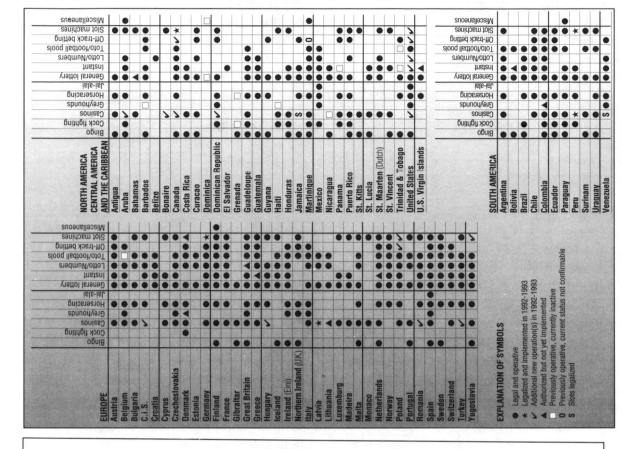

Source: International Gaming & Wagering, NY

IMPORTANT NAMES AND ADDRESSES

American Greyhound Track Operators Association
1065 NE 125 St.
Suite 219
North Miami, FL 33161-5832
(305) 893-2101
FAX (305) 893-5633

American Quarter Horse Association
1600 Quarter Horse Drive
Amarillo, TX 79168
(806) 376-4811
FAX (806) 376-8364

Association of Racing Commissioners
International, Inc.
Kentucky Horse Park
4067 Iron Works Pike
Lexington, KY 40511
(606) 254-4060
FAX (606) 233-4634

Colorado Division of Gaming
720 South Colorado Blvd.
Denver, CO 80222
(303) 757-7555
FAX (303) 757-8624

Compulsive Gambling Center, Inc.
924 East Baltimore St.
Baltimore, MD 21202-4739
(800) 332-0402

Council on Compulsive Gambling
of New Jersey, Inc.
1315 West State St.
Trenton, NJ 08618
(609) 599-3299
1-800-GAMBLER
FAX (609) 599-9383

Gamblers Anonymous
International Service Office
P.O. Box 17173
Los Angeles, CA 90017
(213) 386-8789

Gaming and Wagering Business
BMT Publications
Seven Penn Plaza
New York, NY 10001-3900
(212) 594-4120
FAX (212) 714-0514

Harness Tracks of America
22 Pea Pack Road
P.O. Box 931
Far Hills, NJ 07931
(908) 234-9300
FAX (908) 234-1702

Harrah's Casino Hotels
1023 Cherry Road
Memphis, TX 38117
(901) 762-8790

National Association of Fundraising
Ticket Manufacturers
P.O. Box 2385
Bismarck, ND 58502
(701) 223-1660
FAX (701) 255-6325

National Indian Gaming Association
904 Pennsylvania SE
WDC 20003
(202) 546-7711
FAX (202) 546-1755

National Indian Gaming Commission
1850 M St. NW
Suite 250
WDC 20036
(202) 632-7003
FAX (202) 632-7066

North American Association
of State and Provincial Lotteries
1726 M St. NW
WDC 20036
(202) 223-2423
FAX (202) 833-1577

U.S. Trotting Association
750 Michigan Ave.
Columbus, Oh 43215
(614) 224-2291
FAX (614) 224-4575

State of South Dakota
Commission on Gaming
118 East Missouri
Pierre, SD 57501-5070
(605) 773-6050
FAX (605) 773-6053

RESOURCES

Gambling in America (WDC, 1976), the final report of the Commission on the Review of the National Policy Toward Gambling, despite its age, continues to be the most complete government study on the subject. The Commission requested the Survey Research Center of University of Michigan to prepare an extensive study of gambling. With few exceptions, the Commission accepted the results of that study.

Gaming and Wagering Business, a monthly magazine devoted to the gaming industry, contains invaluable information on every aspect of the industry and periodically publishes special reports on a particular type of gambling activity such as lotteries and casino gambling. Information Plus again extends its sincere appreciation to the magazine for permission to use material from its publications.

The Association of Racing Commissioners International (Lexington, KY) publishes an annual report, *PariMutuel Racing*, that summaries statistics on horse racing, greyhound racing, and jai-alai events. Information Plus would like to thank the Association for permission to use material from their publication.

The American Greyhound Track Operators Association (North Miami, FL) annually publishes *Track Facts* and the *Summary of State Pari-Mutuel Tax Structures* which focus on state taxing and revenue structure and greyhound racing. The *Official Handbook of the American Quarter Horse Association* provides an overview of quarter horse racing in America.

Nevada and New Jersey each publishes a detailed yearly report on casino gambling in their state. The *Nevada Gaming Abstract* is put out by the State Gaming Control Board (Carson City, NV), while the New Jersey Casino Control Commission (Trenton, NJ) issues an *Annual Report*. Both publications provide complete statistical information on casino gambling in those states.

Although not yet in as complete a form as the reports prepared by the gambling commissions of Nevada and New Jersey, the South Dakota Commission on Gaming (Pierre, SD) and the Colorado Division of Gaming (Denver, CO) both release short reports on gambling activities in their states.

The National Association of Fundraising Ticket Manufacturers (NAFTM) (Bismarck, ND) annually surveys bingo, charity gaming, raffles and other forms of gambling. Information Plus would like to thank the NAFTM for permission to use material from its annual *Report on Charity Gaming in North America*.

The Federal Bureau of Investigation maintains statistics on gambling arrests in its annual *Uniform Crime Reports — Crime in the United States*. As always, Information Plus would like to express its sincere appreciation to the Gallup Poll (Princeton, NJ) and the National Opinion Research Center at the University of Chicago (IL) and the Roper Center for Public Opinion Research at the Universityof Connecticut for permission to use material from their surveys.

The *Harrah's Survey of U.S. Casino Gaming Entertainment* (Memphis, TN) is the first national study to "identify how people feel about casino gaming and to develop a profile of who games in casinos, where they visit and what they like to play." The majority of the findings are based on a survey questionnaire developed by the Home Testing Institute (NYC) plus questions commissioned by Harrah's as part of the Yankelovich Clancy Shulman *Monitor*, an annual national survey of human behavior, and interviews conducted by the Communication Development Company (West Des Moines, IA).

Information Plus would also like to thank The Council on Compulsive Gambling of New Jersey, Inc. and Arnie Wexler, the organization's Executive Director for permission to use material from the survey, *New Jersey Residents' Attitudes and Behavior Regarding Gambling,* prepared by the Gallup Organization, Inc. and for other materials prepared by the Council and Mr. Wexler.

The Luxor, Las Vegas, Treasure Island at the Mirage, and the Excalibur Hotel kindly supplied the pictures of their casinos used on the cover.

INDEX